WHAT PEOPLE ARE SAYING ABOUT THIS BOOK

"I've read all thirteen books written by John Irving. This is nowhere near as good as any of them." ~Tom Nagel

"Ten years? It took you ten years to write this? Seriously?" ~Rock Fuqua

"I'm fairly certain most of it is true." ~Greg Retter

"Well, at least the first chapter was pretty good." ~Susan Bennett

"A Tour de Force. Retter's words flow like a leaky faucet." ~Alan Rench

"Hemingway, Faulkner, Steinbeck. I guess they all started somewhere." ~ANON

"I thought it was a little better than *Bleachers* by John Grisham. NOT!" ~Mike Diener

Growing up

a Small-Town Hoosier

Pat,

Enjoy the read!

Greg Cutter

5/6/17

Growing up
a Small-Town Hoosier

Musings of Growing up in the '60s and '70s in Indiana

A Mémoire

GREG RETTER

Johnny & Lois Press

Growing Up a Small-Town Hoosier

Greg Retter

ISBN-13: 978-0692846803
ISBN-10: 0692846808
Library of Congress Control Number: 2017902431

Johnny & Lois Press
5442 White Willow Court
Indianapolis, IN 46254

This book is manufactured in the United States of America.

Editor: Janet Schwind
Designer: Suzanne Parada

CONTENTS

THIS BOOK IS DEDICATED TO
JOHNNY AND LOIS RETTER.
"THE BEST"

WITH SPECIAL THANKS TO

Chuck Huffman
Mike Diener
Connie Retter
Susan Bennett
Oma Scruggs

Downtown Dunkirk

The Phone Call

IT WAS A BALMY MONDAY morning in June like any other. I can't remember what I was doing, but I picked up the phone and the voice on the other end was saying something like, "Mom's ill and they're taking her to the hospital." It was my sister. Thoughts began racing through my head. *This is not good news* and *What should I do?* and, selfishly, *There goes my Monday.* Not knowing exactly what to do next, I simply did nothing, thinking things would take care of themselves. Fifteen minutes later, my sister called again, "You need to come home. This is pretty serious." I didn't have the luxury to do nothing anymore. My attitude changed immediately and I said to my sister, "I'm leaving right now. I'll be there in an hour and a half."

Driving to Muncie was a familiar trip. I'd made the journey many times and this one seemed like the others for the most part. Although not knowing what was going on with my mom, I was a bit more apprehensive, but the 70-mile drive north on I 69 was, thankfully, uneventful. I pulled into the hospital I had come to know so well; my father had been a patient there a few years back for heart bypass surgery. My mother had been on kidney dialysis at a facility adjacent to Ball Hospital and I'd met her and my father there periodically when I could coordinate business calls in the Muncie area. This was not new territory.

I was not prepared, however, for what I would find when I arrived at the hospital. My sister told me Mom was in the cardiac care unit and I found it with the help of a very friendly receptionist. I'll never forget the feeling when I walked into Mom's hospital room and saw her incubated, on a respirator, and unconscious. My lungs deflated. I couldn't catch my breath. My legs buckled under me and I had to sit down. Then I began to cry. I had never seen my mother like this before. I knew immediately that things were serious.

In front of me was a 77-year-old woman who had been with me my entire life. Who'd been my rock, who was always there for me. Someone I could always ask for advice. Oh sure, our conversations of late seemed to migrate toward the weather, or aches and pains. Or of my mother and father's latest trips, or lack thereof. But she was my mother and even the simplest and mundane of contact was important. And cherished.

As a respected and admired citizen of Dunkirk, the small Indiana town where we grew up, my mother was the matriarch of the James family and her five living siblings. A well-read, intelligent, trusted, admired, and wise woman, she was the one who always headed up the family get-togethers and church socials. She was the one you could go to for advice. She loved her family but, as with many Midwestern families, expressed it through her actions instead of her words. And here she was now, lying helpless and in a coma surrounded by my sister, my father, and me.

Details were sketchy about what had happened. My father

was in a daze. He repeated the story many times about how she'd been standing next to the bed, said she didn't feel well, and that she sat down and then fell backwards onto the bed. Each time my father told the story he started tearing up and said with a broken voice, "And there's nothing I could do; if I could have just helped her."

Daily trips to the hospital to see my mother became the norm, and each day the room overflowed with friends, relatives and love. The kindness of my aunts and uncles taught me so much about their compassion and concern for my sister and me. The epicenter of it all, my mother—now on a ventilator, eyes closed, no movement—looked all of her 77 years of age. Nurses and my Aunt Sharon would take turns rubbing her feet. We would huddle around her, taking our turns in a one-sided intimate conversation as she lay motionless. I would sit and read the paper to her, hoping a familiar voice would bring her back. Every day at about the same time, Mother opened her eyes for a few seconds with a glassy stare. Once, and I truly believe this to be true, she looked directly into my eyes and I know she could tell who I was. When she opened her eyes, I would always tell her "Come back to us...we miss you...we need you."

Though it would never produce the desired outcome, the time spent at my mother's side was, in a way, soothing. It allowed us to begin the grieving process. To say goodbye. My 78-year-old father, the respected patriarch, the big guy with the funny disposition, the great stories, sat dejected in a chair with his cane between his knees, staring into space, his eyes and gestures etched with sorrow. He was a broken man not knowing what to do. He looked to me for help—what to ask the doctors, what to say to others. My father had been my inspiration, my role model, the authority figure, my hero, and our leader. He was now the one looking for leadership. And I was now the parent.

During my mother's hospital stay and afterward, I would stay with my father on weekends in his house and sleep in my old bed. Adjacent to my old room and just beyond the wall, my father lay in his bed at night, the sound of his quiet sobs drifting through the emptiness of the old house and piercing my heart. I felt helpless.

Living through the pain and sorrow of my mother's illness had left me weakened and wounded. And it in no way prepared me for the shock of losing her. Though I'd written a eulogy for her years earlier, I was unprepared when the time came. Watching your parent suffer and deteriorate does not ready you for their death. Instead, I was numb and needed to be guided through the motions of grief out of necessity—or survival. What it did for me, however, was to begin the process of opening my mind to a lot of emotions and memories that had been buried, thoughts I'd never examined before. Like where I came from. How I became the person I am. And what influenced my life leading up to that point.

My Hometown of Dunkirk

High School Band impromptu parade

I WAS BORN IN 1954 in a small hospital in Portland, Indiana, a town of about 6,500. I remember visiting the hospital as a child and sensing its antiseptic odor, its long hallways and curious looking rooms with large windows. I don't remember much about my birth as I was busy screaming and gasping for my first breath of oxygen and my eyes were shut, but I assume it was routine. The hospital has since been torn down and a larger, more modern structure has taken its place.

Portland is about fourteen miles from my hometown of Dunkirk, located in east central Indiana and about fifty-five miles south of Fort Wayne. A small community of about 2,500 people, Dunkirk was settled by two brothers-in-law, Isaiah Sutton and William Shrack, who heard (after doing a Google search, I assume) about a congressional act passed in 1820 allowing people to buy public lands for cash. They purchased over 150 acres each, moved to their new properties in 1837, and named the small settlement Quincy, an area located next to the newly built railroad that stretched from Union City, Indiana, to Marion, Indiana.

After Indiana postal officials informed the people of Quincy (I assume via letter instead of e-mail) that a city in Indiana already had that name, settlers changed the name to Dunkirk and county commissioners approved the change.

In 1886 natural gas was discovered in the area and what a boom it was. Gas wells sprung up all over east central Indiana and in 1887 the first well was established in Dunkirk. It's said that Dunkirk was located on one of the strongest gas flows, atop a hump or crown, and the city was nicknamed the Crown City.

The population swelled to 4,500 people in 1894 and businesses thrived, with most of the downtown's buildings springing up at this time. Dunkirk bustled with hotels, boarding houses, saloons, meat markets, an opera house, and many more businesses and professional people. At the height of the boom there were seven glass factories, including four window glass factories, and three others manufacturing bottles, containers, and tableware.

The railroad was the center of activity in early Dunkirk with the interurban line established in 1906. The interurban line had direct lines to the local towns of Muncie, Portland, Albany, and Redkey and could be used to get just about anywhere in the state of Indiana.

The older I get, the more interested I am in this type of historical information, but I remember studying Indiana History and the history of Dunkirk as a youngster while throwing spitballs and staring out the window in utter boredom. Perhaps now, I felt a renewed drive to discover the places and people who helped shaped my life.

The Neighborhood

AS A CHILD IN THE early 1960s, the scope of my world was limited to my house, my yard, a few neighbors' yards, my relatives' houses, and vacation experiences. My earliest memories revolve around the construction of our house on Broad Street. My father hired two of his friends, Bill Boltz and Dick Ford, to build our house, a ranch style with three bedrooms and two bathrooms and a carport with a storage area we called a "shanny" and a basement.

Though I was just four years old and don't remember much about the specific construction process, I have quite vivid memories of the mountains of dirt the process created in front of the house. Atop these massive piles, we spent endless hours playing with our new neighbor friends, Rex and Randy Miller and Jim, Sharon and Karen Shumaker. Ascending the treacherous trails, depleted of oxygen, we'd breathlessly beat our chests and proclaim our victory upon reaching its lofty summit, proud of our accomplishment. The largest mound of dirt stood majestically right in the front of the house with a secondary shorter mound, "the foothill," to the south. The mountains took their substance as a result of the massive hole dug for the new house's basement. At four years old, and being a boy, climbing these dirt mountains was absolutely one of the coolest things you could do.

I've often wondered if the adventure of climbing these dirt mountains didn't influence my interest in climbing later in life. While in my late forties I got the bug to climb Mount Rainier, the largest glaciated mountain in the lower forty-eight states. I signed up for a guided three-day climb, including one day of training, which taught the proper use of an ice ax, how to self-arrest in case you fall, proper use of crampons and ropes, and how to properly pace yourself. Another time I felt compelled to travel to Colorado to climb Long's Peak, a 14,000-footer. There were other climbing adventures, too, including a trip to Alaska to climb several peaks in the Kenai Peninsula, more trips to Colorado to climb smaller mountains, and a trip to the Grand Canyon for a "backwards climb," descending to the bottom through Supai to the Havasu Falls and returning to the top.

Mountains of glorious dirt

In Dunkirk, new house construction on mostly undeveloped land at the edge of town created unexpected benefits and opportunities for a young lad such as myself. The area behind the house consisted mostly of dense woods in development for other homes. Barbier Street was being etched through the woods, and this meant piles of trees, stumps, and limbs on which mischievous, adventurous young boys could play.

My new neighborhood friends

We built forts within the fallen trees and Rex and Randy Miller were particularly good at finding just the right place to make a "kid nest" or fort. One day, for some reason, one of us got hold of some matches. I'm guessing it was Rex as he was about four years older than Randy and me and a bit more mischievous. In a moment of brilliance, we decided to build a small fire within the maze of fallen tree limbs. Little did we know about the dangerous properties of fire at that age and that we could start one, but had no idea of how to put it out. I remember panicking as the flames got a little bigger, not knowing what to do, and Randy and I started to run away. Rex, on the other hand, utilized his more maturely instincts and extinguished the fire with surefire accuracy by peeing on it.

Our new house sprung up between two existing homes like a new finger on a hand. To the north stood a beautiful two-story home, probably built in the forties. To the south, the house where Rex and Randy Miller lived, more of a two-story farm house variety. Our houses skirted the edge of town, in an area where homes were built in the '40s and '50s as the glass industry in town was still going full blast. Business people, factory engineers and managers populated the nearby area. "Alkie" Shumaker owned a plumbing business in downtown Dunkirk. "Skud" Miller worked at the glass factory. George Fulkerson worked at Warner Gear in Muncie. Al Diener was a chemical engineer and assistant manager at the local glass factory. I knew these men because I knew and ran around with their kids, Jim Shumaker, Rex and Randy Miller, Bruce and Craig Fulkerson, and Mike Diener. My world revolved around 420 South Broad Street and I knew little beyond a radius of about an eighth of a mile. Fortunately, there was plenty to do in my little plot of earth, and I was hardly ever bored because of the multitude of adventures at hand.

Our new home with Karen, Connie, and Sharon

It wasn't until later in life that I put two and two together to understand how my father could afford building such a nice new ranch house on the edge of town when he was only in his twenties. His father, my grandfather Roy Retter, had passed away in 1951 at age 53 of a heart attack. Grandpa Roy was delivering taxes to a customer in March and as he walked to exit the door, he slumped over a table and died. Roy attended Tri State College in Angola, Indiana, for a year and business college in Fort Wayne. He had managed a Shell gas station in Dunkirk across the street from Stewart Brothers furniture store. He ran a tax preparation business on the side. His obituary in the newspaper is headed by "Prominent Man Dies Suddenly" and goes on to say, "The entire community was saddened by the sudden death of Roy Retter, prominent local tax accountant." I would think my father and my grandmother were devastated when this happened, and it's funny — my father never talked too much about it. What a tough thing it would be to lose your father when you're just 23 years old.

In every picture I've seen of Grandpa Roy, he was always neatly dressed in either a snappy looking one piece coverall at the gas station or a three-piece suit and tie in family pictures. I've always regretted not meeting or knowing my grandfather, but from what I've been told by those who knew him, he was a "good guy" and "well liked," descriptions I heard often about other Retter great uncles and cousins I never had the opportunity to meet. Seems we were a family full of likeable folk.

Grandpa Roy, Grandma Marjorie, Mom and Dad

Four years later, in 1955 at the age of 55 my grandmother, Marjorie, died of complications from diabetes when I was just a few months old. I never knew my grandmother but the stories I've heard were that she was well liked and had many friends. She was particularly close to her sister Lillian, my great aunt, who I spent much time with as a youngster and who I still refer to as my "surrogate grandmother," as my father and mother spent much time visiting them when I was young.

My grandmother Marjorie was the third of four children of Lysander Stewart, the four children being Denzel, Don, Marjorie, and Lillian. Lysander was the owner of Stewart Brothers Furniture store, a thriving business in Dunkirk. It had opened in 1897 and had been a staple in the community since then. Stewart Brothers Furniture was run by Don and Denzel until sometime in the late '40s or early '50s when there was reportedly a "falling out." Denzel left the Dunkirk store and opened stores in Daleville, Marion and Fairmount, and there continues to be questions about what really happened between Don and Denzel to cause such a family rift. Nevertheless, each continued in the furniture business, creating quite successful ventures apart from each other. I never met Denzel but have since met his children and grandchildren and I'm sure I would have liked him as well.

And so, both of my father's parents passed away within about four years of each other, and at early ages. In 1955, my father, mother, sister and I initially moved into my grandparent's house on North Street behind Calvary Methodist Church, where we lived for a few years while my father made plans for the new house. He then used the life insurance money he'd received and the equity in the house on North Street to build the new house on Broad Street, the place where I would grow up and come to cherish.

Neighborhood Adventure on Broad Street

IF YOU WERE A KID living in Dunkirk in the late fifties and early sixties, and you lived on Broad Street, well, you had it made as far as adventure goes. My earliest memories of when we first moved to Broad Street feature our neighbors Karen, Sharon, and Jim Shumaker and Rex and Randy Miller—my adventure mates. Kick the can was one of our favorite games, which consisted of everyone but one person hiding and the placement of an empty tin can in a central location—and usually played under the cover of darkness. One person was "it" and everyone else ran away and hid. The one who was "it" would try to find those hiding before the hiders could sneak back and kick the can.

Oftentimes you'd have to look up to find us, filling the trees like wild monkeys. We had a huge, beautiful maple tree in our front yard—perfect for gazing at its stunning fall foliage, though not so perfect for climbing. It was very difficult to get into the main or primary limbs because they were so high and the limbs so large. This did not stop us, however, as we employed our monkeylike skills to proudly stake our own spot among its branches. Rex and Randy Miller's property had several trees in their yard that were mature and a bit more accessible, so when we needed an easier climb that was our choice. Each of us had our own "designated" tree, and so we would occasionally climb our individual trees and hang out.

Climbing that massive tree

Opportunities for adventure abounded in my neighborhood on Broad Street. I credit this not so much to the location or the physical landscape, but mainly to all the neighborhood friends close to my age who filled out my childhood experience. However, the biggest, coolest thing we had access to in the neighborhood was the Pine Patch—it fully deserves to be capitalized. The Pine Patch was the magical home and property owned by Al and Aurelia Diener. Spanning several glorious acres, it contained a myriad of features including an orchard with pear and a variety of apple trees, a grape arbor, a section with pine trees, an open meadow for playing baseball, two large sand piles, a big driveway with a basketball goal and the coolest thing of all, a pond.

Now the pond was not very deep; many parents must have been thankful for this. In fact, it would sometimes dry up in the summer. When it was holding water, though, it did support life—some small bluegills—although I'm not sure how they survived from year to year. The most memorable thing about the pond, however, was that it had crawdads (crayfish to some) and enough water to float a boat. Mike Diener, Al's son, who was two years older than me, initially had a little blue plastic boat we would take out onto the pond on sunny days. We'd take a bucket and fish for crawdads, and generally, just think we were the coolest things on earth by having our nautical independence. But the most fun we had on the pond was in the winter when it would freeze.

All the neighbors would congregate at Dieners' pond for ice skating. Everyone owned figure skates (I don't ever remember anyone having hockey skates) and we weren't picky about how we looked. Just bundle us up and give us a pair of skates—even if they were too big, or girl's skates, or whatever—and we would have a blast.

As we got older and slightly more mature, we graduated to playing hockey on the pond. We'd shovel the snow and make a hockey rink per our perceived specifications. Most kids had hockey sticks, but for those who didn't, they'd have to march out into the woods and borrow a suitable stick from Mother Nature. Hockey pucks? Sure, we had 'em, but periodically they would be flung out into the snow, never to be recovered. I remember several times using an old can as a hockey puck and as the game wore on, the can would be reduced to a mangled piece of crushed tin—eventually unusable. Sometimes a snow shovel would fill the role of stick by the goalie. One time during a very heated hockey match, Kane Smith was playing goalie and was using a snow shovel as a hockey stick. Unfortunately, during the match, he didn't have the shovel turned upside down and when he attempted to block a shot on goal, the puck ricocheted up the curve of the shovel, smacking him squarely in his face. Luckily, he wasn't seriously injured and we most likely continued with the game—only stopping if someone appeared dead.

Al and Aurelia Diener were wonderful neighbors and amazing people, loved by all. Al worked at Armstrong Cork, a maker of bottles, and was a Purdue graduate. Aurelia was a homemaker and mother to six children. Just outside the entrance to their house was a very large bell on a post. When it was time for Mike to come home or for him to come in from the pond, Aurelia would ring that bell—the familiar sound heard 'round the neighborhood. During the very rare times that we were inside their house (there were way too many things to do outside), Aurelia would bring out an elegantly presented tray containing colorful aluminum glasses full of water and an assortment of "Fizzies" tablets, which we put into water and drank. Her hostessing skills dazzled us. I wasn't used to having drinks served to me on a tray and the aluminum glasses were memorable because

I'd never seen anything like them before. I imagine aluminum glasses were a bit more practical, and safe, considering Aurelia had already raised five children and was now experiencing her sixth, a young and rambunctious son Mike who brought along his cronies for a snack while taking a break from playing.

As I got older, my adventures turned more to competitive sports and less playing army at the Pine Patch and hunting crawdads in the pond. We were old enough to play basketball and basketball we played. To our delight, almost every house in the neighborhood had a basketball backboard and rim. Dieners had one, I had one, Fulkersons had one, (Fred) Finches had one. We seemed to go over to Betty and George Fulkerson's house the most, however. The reason, I think, was due to the nice flat cement surface of their driveway and its location being a bit more central. Betty and George were probably used to having boys over since they had three boys of their own. Two of them, my pals Craig and Bruce, lived two houses down the street from me around the corner on Moore Avenue and we'd pick up Randy Miller or Bill Mizner for a little game of two on two. It was a year 'round all-weather addiction—in the summer sun, sometimes in the rain, and many times in the winter when we had no trouble shoveling the snow off the driveway and wearing gloves to keep our game on. Our love of the game was so intense I remember once wearing a hole in the right finger of my glove from playing so much.

Baseball was another of our favorite pastimes and next to Fred Finch's house on Moore Avenue was a vacant lot where we'd have games of three-on-three hard ball. To this day, I can't understand how we never destroyed anything in our zeal for the sport. The lot with our baseball diamond was sandwiched between Ludwig's house on one side and Finch's on the other—so there wasn't much room for error. The homerun area was the woods and right behind home plate was Moore Avenue. So, by my scientific calculations, we must've either hit all home runs or struck out to avoiding hitting any houses. Baseball was fun, but basketball was truly our game.

Household Chores and Jobs

WHEN I ACHIEVED THE MYSTERIOUS "boy of a certain age" status, I was assigned a new thing called household chores. I believe chores are typically designed to ruin a young man's childhood, but my parents were not good at that because I really liked my chore. The first chore I had was to take discarded tin cans, remove the lids, and carry them downstairs to the basement. Then I was to place the cans on the cement floor and, using a rubber-headed hammer, flatten the cans and then place them into our "incinerator," a rather rudimentary appliance about the size of a dishwasher into which we put our trash to be burned. At the time, the flattening of tin cans seemed to be a very important function, to me anyway. To this day, I'm not sure if the job was truly of a critical nature, or just something to help a young boy to become responsible. I enjoyed the job as it made me feel important and allowed me to use a hammer and deal destruction to something—which, I assume, is something all young boys enjoy.

My sister and I would also be responsible for washing dishes after supper. We alternated each week and I am sorry if this sounds sexist, but it was not exactly a popular job for a young boy, who would much rather be playing outside than standing by the sink cleaning off dishes. I recall my mother pointing out to me that the job I was doing was a bit less than adequate as I was not being thorough. My response, which I thought rather clever, was, "Okay, FIRE me!" Mom's reaction was always good natured and she most likely said something like, "You, sir, just need more practice!"—which she was always glad to provide the opportunity for. My mother, sister, and I told this story for years and years.

Later, I graduated to the manly task of mowing the lawn, and it was here that I learned a valuable lesson. We had two lawn-mowers—a small yellow Lawnboy and a somewhat larger tan colored Lawnboy. We used the smaller one to mow under and around the pine trees in the yard, as it was easier to maneuver. We used the larger one for the main part of the yard. Sometimes my father would mow at the same time as me and we would need to carefully choreograph our mowing paths so as not to run into each other.

My mother always loved to garden and always planted flowers around the yard light and next to the front yard patio. She particularly liked impatiens and marigolds and would occasionally plant something different. One year she planted something exotic, which I now know as Allium Giganteum, a bulb with a gorgeous purple spherical bloom and a long narrow stock that sometimes grows to 39 inches in height. I was probably thirteen years old and as a "future track and basketball star," as I liked to label myself, I would mow the grass as quickly as I could, simulating a workout and minimizing time spent working so I could do more important things like playing basketball or watching TV. In the process, I carelessly mowed over one of the two beautiful Alliums and didn't think much of it. Unfortunately, my mother thought very much of it, and told me such. I had no idea, as a naive, immature, thoughtless youngster, how important this flower was, or what pride she took in growing her garden. Surprisingly (and interestingly) I noticed that her reaction was subtle, but effective. I could sense she was very upset with me when she told me how important the flower was, but she didn't raise her voice at me or make a huge deal out of it. That incident stuck with me and thus I learned to be more careful and more respectful of others' possessions.

My mother and father didn't have a full-fledged garden or grow many vegetables in our yard, but we did have a small patch of tomatoes for a few years. We also had several happenstance growths of rhubarb near the back property line. My mother would cut the rhubarb and combine with sugar to make the most delicious rhubarb pie. As youths, we would break a rhubarb stock right off the plant and eat it raw. The tart taste of rhubarb, particularly of the greener stocks, made for a fun, natural snack.

For a few years, my mother took advantage of an empty lot between the Millers' and the Shumakers' houses, which she used to plant a large garden for a few years. The garden contained tomatoes, carrots, sweet corn and a variety of other native Indiana vegetables. The one item I remember we grew one year was turnips and I remember picking them straight from the stem, wiping the dirt off them and eating them like an apple, while standing right there in the garden. I also recall that turnips made my breath smell and that chewing a piece of my mother's Dentyne would be more than welcome.

As I got older and my social life expanded, so too did my need for money; I became markedly more industrious in looking for ways to earn cash. My first job making more than a few pennies was given to me by my father and that job was to paint the exterior of our house. I spent an entire summer painting the dark brown siding of the house and its white windows, trying not to spill drops of paint on the limestone brick accent on its front. I would paint almost every day for an hour or two between times of playing basketball or going to the pool. My pay rate was 35 cents per hour, and I remember meticulously tracking my beginning and ending work time and netting out the difference. When I'd finally completed the job, my father paid me a lump sum, and gave me as a bonus an Electrolux AM/FM radio, complete with eight-track tape player—an appliance that, remarkably, I still have today.

Painting the house, making the big bucks

Not known for my painting prowess, I was later awarded more painting jobs (including a friend of my father's garage) and some additional mowing gigs. My great uncle, Ernest Littler, once hired me to mow the orchard behind his house on Main Street. It was a big lot and took quite a while to complete, but the biggest challenge was dealing with how rough it was—I had gotten so completely worn out from the vibrations of the mower handle that my hands shook. The orchard was located behind where my basketball coach Roy Sneed lived, and I remember thinking he was probably looking out the window at me while I mowed, saying to himself, "Now, that guy works hard. I think he'll be a basketball star." Also added to my résumé was headstone digger when I helped my father dig grave headstone holes a few times as he was the "sexton" at the local cemetery.

I even helped bale hay a few times. Somehow a few of us guys would hear that a farmer south of town was looking to hire young, cheap labor for a crew and that it paid so much per bale. Our job was to follow the baler and pick up the bales off the ground, throw them up onto the wagon, and stack them in a certain fashion to prevent them from falling off. Once the wagon was full, we would take it to a local barn and throw the bales onto a conveyer that took the hay into a small barn. We would stack it as high as we could inside the barn all the way to the ceiling and I remember it was the hottest job I'd ever had since we had to wear long pants, a long sleeve shirt and gloves.

My first real job came when I worked at Stewart Brothers furniture as a delivery man after my graduation from high school. Just prior to that, an interesting thing had happened when the Indiana Glass Factory, the local factory that made decorative glassware, called me out of the blue at home one day to see if I wanted a summer job there. Granted, it was in the furnace area, a job not particularly popular with people, but the fact they called me to offer me a job without me applying for it was surely interesting and something that I'm sure rarely happens even today.

The next few years I worked on the state highway as part of a "college crew." I always liked working outside so this sounded like something right up my alley. Plus, the job was never boring as we would do something different almost every day. Just as you would guess about a government job, there were some days when we stood around doing absolutely nothing and there were other days when we worked our rear ends off and got filthy dirty. I preferred the filthy dirty days, myself.

Traveling and Vacations

SMALL-TOWN LIVING DID HAVE some shortcomings in the 1960s. For instance, one's view of the world could sometimes be quite limited, and while perusing the *World Book* or *Compton's Encyclopedia* (we had a complete edition) is a decent way to learn about the world, it's not necessarily the preferred way to broaden one's horizons.

The Stewart family (my fraternal grandmother's family), however, had an inherent gene which I call an adventure or travel gene. My grandmother Marjorie, great aunt Lillian, great uncle Denzel and great uncle Don all had it. They traveled from Dunkirk, Indiana, to Utah back in 1922 in a 1921 Studebaker touring convertible, camping out along the way because there weren't any motels. Can you imagine that? Traveling a couple of thousand miles through the U.S. on narrow, newly created state highways? Apparently back then, you could get free claim to land in Utah if you showed up and lived on it for a period and that's what my Great Uncle Denzel intended to do. The pictures of them in the Rocky Mountains standing next to the '20s era car with running boards loaded with luggage, tents, etc., is amazing.

When I got older I visited my great Aunt Lillian and Uncle Ernest and sat through their slide shows of pictures taken on their subsequent trips around the country. My strongest memory is that of being bored—out of my flipping mind. Luckily, after accompanying my family on a multitude of trips and continuing with trips on my own later in life, I discovered that watching slide shows and experiencing travel are two very different things.

In the '60s, small-town neighbors tended to be familiar with one another. My mother had "coffee" with Virginia Miller and Evelyn Shumaker frequently and we knew them well. Evelyn lived two houses down the street and was from Petoskey, Michigan. I don't know how she migrated to Dunkirk but she married Ralph "Alkie" Shumaker and they had three children: Karen, Sharon, and Jim. We ended up hanging with the Shumakers frequently and going with them to visit Evelyn's family in the far away, magical land of Petoskey a couple of times. Located in the upper lower peninsula, Petoskey was a winter bazaar. Up there, they ice skated, sledded, and played "curling," a sport I'd never seen before. We sledded in Dunkirk, primarily by means of being pulled on a "disc" sled down the street behind a station wagon with its rear gate open. By contrast, the sledding in Petoskey on real actual hills was a huge thrill and offered an invigorating adventure.

Over the years, our method of camping during family vacations evolved from initially sleeping in a tent, to having a very small Shasta trailer, to sleeping in a bit larger Holiday Rambler trailer. The trailers afforded us the ability to be self-contained while taking a lot more stuff with us. It was always cool pulling into a park and setting up camp, excited and anticipating the new friends we'd make and the adventures ahead of us. Campgrounds always had lots to do and many places to explore, and I think my father enjoyed the process of leveling the trailer and creating a place for us to live. When we weren't at home, taking care of our "mobile home" was the man's job and my father reveled in it.

In New York City camping in the Holiday Rambler

Our travel destinations included Ludington, Michigan, and Sault Ste. Marie, Michigan, which we visited multiple times. We also traveled to Quebec City, Quebec, and in 1964 and 1965 to the New York City world's fair—quite memorable family adventures. We pulled our trailer to New York City and parked it in a campground with a gravel surface. We would catch a bus right near the campground, which would then take us to the subway, which would take us to the fair, located in Flushing Meadows, New York.

We also visited Washington, DC, and made the trek out to Colorado to visit old friends and relatives, including Dad's cousin Ernie and Virginia Littler who lived in Golden. Ernie was a year younger than my father, attended Dunkirk High School and served as my father's best man when he got married. I was always told they were good friends while growing up and I've always regretted not visiting Ernie later in life.

The most memorable vacation I can remember was our three-week trip out west when we visited Mount Rushmore, the Badlands in South Dakota, Yellowstone National Park, Salt Lake City, the Great Salt Lake, Reno Nevada, Death Valley, San Francisco, Los Angeles (Disneyland and Knott's Berry Farm), the Grand Canyon, and the Painted Forest of Arizona. What an amazing trip and to think, we traveled all that distance in our Ford Galaxy 500 station wagon before the interstate road network had been completed and without air conditioning or cell phones or mini TV screens in our car. All in all, an impressive résumé of travel for a young kid from a small town.

My parents proudly carried on this tradition of the Stewart "travel" gene and after us kids had grown, ended up visiting all 50 states after completing a cruise to Alaska and a brief vacation to Honolulu. They always loved visiting Charleston, South

Carolina, and it was sad when they could no longer go on the bus trips with those other "old people" because of their failing health. My sister and I, however, have proudly continued the legacy; I've completed two trips to Europe and visited South and Central America, as well as all 50 states. My sister has done multiple "cruises" and she and I have visited "long lost" cousins in California, Cape Cod, and Arizona and hope to keep traveling as one of our retirement priorities.

Chapman Lake on the Weekends

WHEN I WAS A YOUNGSTER our family had a place at "the lakes," which was on Little Chapman Lake in northern Indiana, situated between Warsaw and North Webster. Our place was a house trailer situated amongst a bunch of other house trailers in an area known as Lozier's Park. The trailer sat on a channel that gave us access to Little Chapman Lake, a lake that didn't allow speedboats but was linked to Big Chapman Lake via a channel. Big Chapman Lake allowed speedboats. For this, I was glad.

Lozier's Park was home to many Dunkirk residents who trekked to "the lakes" on the weekend and it was almost a home away from home. We got to know some other families at the lakes and hung out a lot with Bond and Pat Stanley who were from Redkey, a town five miles from Dunkirk, and who had a trailer a few lots down from ours. Their son Ted and I were about the same age, so we fished together, boated together and played basketball on the small gravel basketball court located just east of the channel.

The Stanleys had a pontoon boat and we would use it to go crappie fishing at night. Sometimes we'd take our speedboat and their pontoon boat to Big Chapman Lake, and use the pontoon as an observation point for those not wanting to ride in the speedboat, but who wanted to watch those who water skied.

At the lakes, we were fortunate to have a plethora of entertainment and boating options at our disposal. In addition to the Stanleys' pontoon, we had a fiberglass StarCraft inboard/outboard speedboat for skiing, a twelve-foot sailboat for sailing, and a ten foot Johnny boat for fishing. My father made the sailboat and constructed it in his workshop in the basement of our house. I still remember the jokes as to whether the completed boat would fit through the storm door exit leading to the basement. Luckily, it did and we transported it proudly to the lakes.

Sailing on Little Chapman Lake with Uncle Gary

At Big Chapman Lake, our skiing adventures usually consisted of one outing on Saturday and one on Sunday. Everyone skied, except for my mother and father. My mother didn't even get into the water as she didn't like it and most likely couldn't swim as she hadn't grown up around water. Our speedboat was adequately powered, but it still took some effort to pull people out of the water. My poor sister took a while to learn how to ski. She worked hard at "getting up" out of the water on two skis and eventually figured it out but she would always remain directly behind the boat, never venturing over the wake into unchartered (fun) territory.

As we got more talented at skiing, we would try to slalom ski. It required a momentous effort—not to mention great athletic skill—to pull oneself out of the water on a single slalom ski. After being pulled by the boat for a significant length and by the time you could get yourself upright after many failed attempts, your arms were usually "trashed" and you could only ski for a short time. Due to the difficulty of being pulled out of the water on a slalom ski in a timely fashion led to an easier process whereby we would start our skiing on two skis and kick one off, near the shallows where boats tended not to venture. Cheating? Maybe. But it worked for us!

Skiing on Big Chapman Lake

Fishing was a popular pastime with us, and fly fishing was my favorite — this type of fishing particularly fit my personality. With fly fishing, you are busy all the time ... casting and retrieving the line constantly... looking for just that right spot to place the fly near a downed tree or lily pad or shady spot... wiggling the fly on the retrieval just enough to create movement so that the fish will see it. I was a "dry" fly fisherman, which meant my flies floated on the surface as I loved to see the fish "hit" the fly and pull the line in, one handful of line at a time, while my fly pole doubled over to accommodate the (usually) tiny bluegill or rock bass. I also discovered I preferred flies that looked like spiders, preferably light green or white, instead of "popper" flies, which were constructed of wood and made a sound when you retrieved them from the water.

I spent untold hours walking out on rickety wooden piers along the channel and practicing my fly fishing technique. Fly fishing requires a bit of talent and timing and I never seemed to have a problem picking up its idiosyncrasies. I enjoyed the solitude and independence of taking my Johnny boat out into Little Chapman Lake among the lily pads and cattails and stand up in the boat, casting for bluebill and rock bass amid the buzzing of the large Indiana dragonflies and the gentle lapping of water against the side of my boat.

In the evenings after a full day being outdoors, we ventured into town, usually North Webster and sometimes Warsaw. North Webster had all kinds of activities for kids and we would play miniature golf, jump on the trampolines, shop, or get an ice cream cone.

Growing up at "the lakes" was a wonderful experience and suddenly (or what felt like suddenly) when I was a senior in high school, my father and Uncle Gary decided to sell the place and it all came to a screeching halt. It felt significant and a bit sad—it was the end of an era. I think they realized that times were changing and that my sister and I were entering a different stage of life, that we'd lost interest in going and had our sights set on other activities now, which for me was going to college. As a youngster, I don't think I appreciated what a wonderful resource we had at the lakes or how the experiences there helped shape me as a person. I have so many great memories of being there, and it helped me realize that there were places other than Dunkirk where I could feel safe, and have fun, and meet other people, and experience physical activities other than playing basketball, playing army, and ice skating. It had opened another world to me.

Scouts and Camp

WHEN I WAS ABOUT EIGHT years old, my parents enrolled me in Cub Scouts. This was another way that my parents gave me adventures that would shape who I was, and help me grow in confidence. We attended pack meetings at Mary Ann Wise's house on Main Street. Mary Ann and Betty Fulkerson were our den leaders. Now that I think about this, I marvel that we had female den leaders back then. Maybe we were ahead of our time. Working our way through the Cub Scout Manual, my brother scouts and I systematically performed the required tasks and activities to earn ourselves the various badges of achievement. My sister had her own thing going on too as my mom enrolled her in Brownies.

Cub Scout Greg

The biggest activity we were involved in was the annual pinewood derby. Held at the American Legion, the derby used a long wooden track that accommodated, I believe, three cars at a time and was probably 25 feet long. It would be interesting to know where this track came from or who built it as it was quite elaborate and had to be built per specifications. Each scout received a "kit" used to build their car, which consisted of a block of pine wood with a notch cut out for the cockpit, four plastic wheels, four nails used for axles, and two smaller pieces of wood in which to put the axles. As you might guess, the construction of the pinewood derby cars was left mostly to the fathers of each scout. This was blatantly obvious if you looked at the level of construction detail on the cars—and then looked at the little boys who had allegedly built them. Most of the dads were obviously handy with their hands or familiar with the mechanics of basic construction technique. Many fathers worked in trades that included making things (e.g., mold makers at the glass factory) and they knew tricks for making the cars operate smoothly by strategically placing weights on the car's bottoms, or using graphite to lubricate the axles, or to sand down the axles for a smooth rolling wheel. My father utilized his wood-working skills so I had a nice-looking car with smoothly sanded edges, somewhat resembling an Indianapolis 500 roadster from the 1950s.

I did make my mark on the project though: painting the car, for which I selected a sort of British racing green color. Beyond that, my only other responsibility was during the actual derby when I would retrieve my car from the table containing all the scouts' cars and carrying it to the derby starting line when my name was called. Once the lever was pulled to release the cars at the race's start, there was much cheering and yelling and discussions as to whether one lane was faster than the others as it seemed most winners came from that lane. I didn't win the derby or even place, but the best part for me was working alongside my father on a project. It also taught me how to compete with others and learn about sportsmanship, and that not everyone can win.

After a couple of years, I was old enough to graduate from Cub Scout to Boy Scout and I started attending Boy Scout meetings in the "Scout Cabin" on West Commerce Street. Richard Whitesell, a friendly, dedicated man with three boys of his own, was our Boy Scout leader, and our objectives turned to earning "merit badges" so that we could climb the ladder of scouting ranks.

Being in Boy Scouts and being a bit older opened the door for more advanced adventures. One time our scout troop went on a camping outing and we walked, er, hiked about two miles south of Dunkirk and camped in a field just off a county road. We had a campfire, played Taps and Reveille, and cooked our food over the fire like real outdoorsmen, most likely "Vienna sausages," a popular delicacy of young men in those days that came in a small can with a pull tab, which, with our sophisticated taste, we considered gourmet food. Another camping trip took us to Frank Merry Park just west of Dunkirk. But the biggest adventure of all was a week-long trip to Boy Scout Camp, Camp Big Island in 1966 and 1967, a place where scouts went to commune with nature and learn more about scouting.

Camp Big Island was an actual island located on Sylvan Lake near Rome City, Indiana, in northern Indiana and was accessible via pontoon boat. We loaded our gear onto the boat, set sail for the island, and became part of a larger congregation of Scout Troops from all over northern Indiana. While there, our days would be filled with activities and working on earning our merit badges. I got merit badges in canoeing and basketmaking. Yes. Really, basketmaking. Several of us made baskets out of wicker under the tutelage of someone, I presume the Grand Basketmaking "Poohbah" of the camp. Later, I took my basket home and proudly presented it to my mother where she displayed it prominently in the living room or kitchen until which time it either fell apart or somehow mysteriously disappeared into a nearby trash receptacle.

I remember participating in an odd, fun contest wherein a greased watermelon was thrown into the water and our team tried to be the first to land the slippery orb onto the beach. The ensuing water frenzy of flailing arms, legs and torsos reminded me of the churning waters created by a shark attack, only ours were screams of laughter rather than terror. We won, by the way. We also had access to swimming and I got my badge for the "one mile swim" by completing the required number of laps between two piers.

One night toward the end of our Big Island retreat we went to a ceremony selecting scouts for the "Order of the Arrow" designation. Order of the Arrow recognized certain scouts who exemplify the scout oath, best maintain camping traditions and spirit, are potential leaders, and provide cheerful service to others. The ceremony was considered very sacred and solemn. We were gathered together in an opening of the woods and were told to stand in a circle looking inward and not say anything. A man appeared wearing Indian garb and started walking slowly, silently, between each scout, stopping briefly to look at each of us in the face with a menacing glare. Suddenly he would stop in front of a scout, look him in the eye, and dramatically slap him on the top of the shoulder once, then quickly, two more times. That scout who was "tapped" had been selected to join the "Order of the Arrow" and followed the Indian into the dark woods for who knows what additional initiation rituals. While standing in the circle I was scared out of my mind hoping the serious, intimidating Indian wouldn't stop in front of me.

At Boy Scout Camp, Big Island

I achieved the rank of First Class during my years in Boy Scouts, which eventually lead to Explorer Scouts when we reached junior high school. In Explorer Scouts, our major expedition consisted of a one-week, 100-mile canoe trip on the White Pigeon River in northern Indiana and southern Michigan. We were self-contained, cooked our own food and camped along the river. Several times we portaged our canoes around a dam—the stuff of manliness. A classmate of my father, John Faris was our leader at the time and I shared a canoe with my neighbor Bruce Fulkerson. I remember the solitude of the trip, truly feeling connected to the outdoors, and then experiencing the sudden disruption the time we stopped along the river to climb the bank to find a small grocery store. It felt so surreal to return to civilization after being isolated for so long, reminding me that this whole other world did not cease to exist if we weren't there. Once we were back in nature, I felt like an explorer again, dealing with challenges like the large spiders hanging from trees that would drop into our canoes. We'd only been gone for one week on that canoe trip, but it seemed like we'd been living in the wilderness forever. I remember the return trip in the van, pulling our canoes on a trailer, took only a couple of hours and we were back in civilization once more.

One moment that will always stand out in my memory happened on our return home. As we sat in our car at the McDonalds on Coliseum Boulevard in Fort Wayne, we listened to the radio as Neil Armstrong and Buzz Aldrin had just landed on the moon. It was July 20, 1969—one of those "where were you when" lifetime events.

I think we always remember our first adventure away from our parents. I was fortunate to attend a trip to Camp Crosley, the YMCA camp on Lake Webster in northern Indiana. I still remember sitting on the bus in Muncie, anxiously awaiting our departure, looking out the window at my mother who had what seemed to me like a "concerned" look on her face. As a naive youngster looking forward to a week of activities with some of my buddies, I had no idea what was going through her mind as she sent off her young son for the first time—but I must assume some of it was fear. I was, after all, a boy. My mother had purchased small cotton name tags from some faraway place with my name on them. She sewed one of these tags on every piece of clothing I took to camp—even my socks. I'm sure this type of thing was manifested from her being the oldest of seven siblings, and more likely her recognizing that young boys have more important things to think about than keeping track of their underwear or that one sock while at camp.

The week's experience went, for the most part, smoothly, with the most memorable and fun part being the communal living with several other like-aged, rambunctious rug rats. We lived in small cottages with bunk beds attached to the inside walls covering the entire inside of the building. Beyond all the usual outdoor activities and crafts of camp life, we were required to be responsible youth. We made our beds daily and cleaned the floors. We were assigned an assortment of responsibilities to help where needed, and anxiously awaited the nightly announcement of the "cleanest cabin" award. When my parents visited later that week, I awkwardly gave them a tour of the grounds and showed them what I had been doing. I was of the age when you want to see your parents, but you don't want the others to see or know how much you had missed them. I tried to keep my cool with a nonchalant air about me. Luckily, I stayed busy enough with activities and had ample buddies to keep me from getting homesick.

Ye Old Swimmin' Holes

ACCESS TO WATER IN LANDLOCKED east central Indiana was surprisingly easy. In addition to my swimming experiences at Camp Crosley, Camp Big Island, and Chapman Lake there were ample opportunities for water mischief and swimming experiences in and around Dunkirk.

Wilson's existed just west of Dunkirk and featured a large pond, a couple of floating docks, and a sandy beach. They also had a snack bar and we would ride our bikes the mile or two to the pond or be dropped off by our parents for an afternoon of frolicking in the water and jumping off the floating docks. The obligatory swimming lessons were also there to be had, a comfort to our parents if nothing else.

In the late 1960s, Dunkirk built a community pool in the city park next to the tennis courts, a welcome addition to the neighborhood. We would put on our bathing suits, gather our beach towel, jump on our bikes and ride the approximately one mile to the pool. The "L" shaped pool consisted of a 25-yard section for open swimming and a smaller area 12-feet deep with a three-foot and a ten-foot diving board. The pool employed a friendly staff of two lifeguards, a snack bar manager, personnel to manage your clothes in baskets stored in the basket room, and a pool manager. The Dunkirk community pool was *the* place to go in the late '60s and '70s, and we would spend much time there playing Marco Polo, tag, and showing off to the girls by diving off the boards. As we got older, our diving became a lot more daring and doing one-and-a-halfs off the low board became easy. Some of us tried to do twos off the lows, but it was a bit too much of a challenge given the stiffness of the diving boards.

The high board was even more challenging and some of my friends got a little daring and talented at doing one-and-a-halfs off it. A few people attempted twos off the high board, but the risk/reward of doing complicated diving didn't quite measure out. I was unsuccessful at doing one-and-a-halfs off the high board a couple of times and my career in that area soon ended. It wasn't worth risking my life and more importantly, my ego, by failing. I could do one-and-a-halfs off the low, but the failure "level of pain" wasn't as great as on the high board and so we continued, particularly when there were girls sunning themselves on the deck.

While in high school. I took a lifeguarding class there, which led to a brief stint as a lifeguard. You'd think that would be a super cool job, saving lives right and left. The reality, however, was much less exciting. Fifty-minute shifts in each chair, separated by a ten-minute break was just about as boring as it gets — even more boring than studying Indiana history.

As we got older, we ventured to swimming holes further

away from Dunkirk and someone discovered a place named Pine Lake. About 30 miles north of Dunkirk, near Berne, Pine Lake *gave* us the opportunity for a road trip adventure. Somehow, the word would get circulated that people were going to Pine Lake and we would car pool. Pine Lake was bigger than Wilson's and had a diving tower with ten-, twenty- and thirty-foot platforms. Now, jumping off the thirty-foot platform was not necessarily a decision you make lightly. Jumping off was the easy part; the hard part was the inevitable pain when your feet collided with the water and your arms were thrusted upward. I'm not sure jumping off the thirty-foot platform was *fun* — more of a challenge and an "I did it" sort of thing. I remember, however, seeing Craig Fulkerson, who was a bit more daring than most of us, do a one-and-a-half forward dive off the thirty-foot platform. A demonstration of courage (or stupidity, depending on how you look at it), the kind of which legends are made.

Family

MY PARENTS WERE JOHN WILLIAM Retter and Lois Jane James Retter. My mother was born in 1929 (at home, the old-fashioned way) and was the oldest of seven children. Her father, Everett James, was a dairy farmer and her mother Nelda, a homemaker. In my early childhood, we spent lots of time at Grandpa James' dairy farm, just a few miles in the country from Dunkirk. Grandpa had between fifteen to twenty Holstein milk cows and I would tag along with him during some of his evening milkings. I was amazed at the clockwork of it—how the cows would just start wandering in at a certain time and automatically know to walk to a certain spot in the barn. My grandfather would then hook their teats up to an automatic milking machine that extracted their milk and deposited it into stainless steel containers.

A farmer's work was more a lifestyle than a job. The cows were milked twice a day, 365 days a year, which meant my grandfather needed to be at the farm every day of his life. This meant all our family dinners were there, too, and sometimes I stayed on the farm on the weekends, too. It was a wondrous place to explore, including the hay barn where we spent hours making forts in the "hay mow" and climbing the hay bales. Grandpa James also had soybeans and wheat stored in large wooden compartments, providing another opportunity for adventure. While the adults stayed inside having conversations, we would venture out and jump into the deep vats, filling our shoes with the grains. We would also climb the ladder on the silo up the darkened tunnel on its side as the pungent smell of the silage filled our nostrils and our memories.

I never remember getting into trouble for being a bit of a mischievous, adventurous lad and I must believe that my grandfather was a grace-filled man, just overlooking what we were doing. Little did we understand that this was his occupation, his business, his way of making a living, and we were fiddling around in it. My sister, cousins Julayne, Terri and Tim were all accomplices in these activities and it was a great way of getting to know them and of having fun.

Weekends visiting grandma and grandpa James' farmhouse meant staying in the sometimes-chilly upstairs bedrooms with squeaky hardwood floors and a single naked lightbulb to illuminate the room, operated by a string hanging down as an on/off switch. I still remember waking up to the smell of breakfast downstairs and hitting the hardwood floor in my bare feet, and making my way downstairs to a breakfast of fried eggs, bacon and toast all served up on a massive wooden kitchen farm table. On Sundays, we'd make our way to the Bethel EUB (Evangelical United Brethren) church for services and Grandma and

Grandpa would always be smack in the front row. We'd go to Sunday School after services and sit downstairs singing songs, listening to Bible stories, and smelling that well-known church basement smell, which was a mixture of musty cement floor and cement block walls, old hymnals, construction paper and paste, folding wooden chairs, candle wax, and years and years of carry-in meals consisting of fried chicken, noodles, mashed potatoes, and a variety and assortment of casseroles.

My grandmother Nelda was the matriarch of the James family and I tell people she was the best cook in the world, having grown up with seven kids on a dairy farm. She made amazing chicken and noodles, pies, just about anything you can think of. I don't think I knew my grandmother's first name until I was probably thirty years old. She lived to be a ripe old 95 and had an amazing clear mind right up until she died in 2001. I visited her a few times in the Albany nursing home just prior to her passing away and she would never complain about a thing, always asking me about what was going on in my life, and she always remembered our conversations from my prior visit. I would occasionally sneak her a milkshake from the Dairy Dream located across the street; she deserved it! She was someone who was always there for all of us, and I'm amazed at what she did as a woman. Raising seven kids on dairy farms. Cooking for her large brood of kids. Washing clothes in that old "mostly manual" Maytag wringer washing machine. Hanging the wash out on the clothesline to dry. Keeping a big farmhouse clean.

In Chicago with Grandma James and Uncle Gary

Later in life when she could still shuffle under her own power but needed to be transported over larger distances in a wheelchair, she told us, unselfishly, not to worry if she couldn't make it to a family gathering because access to the house wasn't wheelchair friendly. We had nothing to do with her statement of humility and selflessness, and my uncles and I happily carried the wheelchair up the stairs and into our house where she could be part of the family get-together.

Two of my mother's siblings, Gary and Joyce, were sort of like big siblings to me. Gary, only eleven years older and Joyce, fourteen years older, hung out with our family a lot until they each got married and started their own families. Joyce went on a couple of Michigan vacations with us. Gary was always the bachelor guy with the pretty cool car. The one I particularly remember was a dark blue Oldsmobile Cutlass S with a four-speed manual transmission and a big engine. Gary was in cahoots with my father in securing a place for us to go on the weekends at Little Lake Chapman in northern Indiana.

On a trip with Aunt Joyce

My other aunts and uncles—Sandy, Larry, Wayne, and Rodger (who sadly was killed in an auto accident in the early '60s)—were always around and when we all got together with them, their spouses, and their kids, created quite a large clan for our family meals. The James family had frequent get-togethers and were (and are) all very good and kind people. Rifts that exist in so many families today didn't exist in ours. I feel truly blessed that we all got along so well, even if I didn't realize back then how unusual this might be. My grandmother's strict rules (she didn't allow playing cards in the house and booze was unthinkable) and loving nature had a lot to do with why we all got along. I think her loving nature was the result of, perhaps, compensating for my grandfather who was always quiet and, as I later learned, stern and a bit difficult on some of his kids (my aunts and uncles).

As with most families, generations seem to move to different geographic locations based on when they were born. My aunts and uncles, born pre-baby boomer (1929-1943), tended to settle closer to where they were brought up and have stayed, mostly, close to Dunkirk. Their children (my cousins) have tended to move a bit further from home, chasing careers or better job opportunities in larger cities.

My sister Connie was three years older than me and, it's funny, but I never really remember fussing or fighting with her. I'm sure it must have happened, but I think there was just enough of an age difference that we pretty much left each other alone. Plus, we had almost polar-opposite interests and activities. I was involved in sports; Connie was involved in the arts. Perhaps it's because women's high school sports in the '60s were pretty nonexistent in our small high school. Only GAA (Girls Athletic Association) existed, and I believe our school just played a few games of basketball among themselves and other nearby schools. When Title IX was established in 1972 it opened the door for women's sports to flourish at the high school and college level.

Reading with Connie

My mother was my rock growing up, the best mom a kid could have hoped for—the epitome of small-town goodness. To me, she stood tall and stood out in her nurturing ways, with a demeanor that was low-key and consistent. A woman of average height with medium brown hair, her complexion was a bit flushed or pale as she never seemed to tan in the summer and carried that same pallid hue throughout the year. Remarkably, her hair color stayed the same medium brown throughout her life, something I'm sure her hair dresser had a part in. In very few pictures over the years do we see her smiling, which did not match her general jovial and lighthearted ways. I always attributed the lack of smiles mostly to her impatience with my father's incessant picture taking. Oddly, after she passed away I had a couple of friends tell me my mother sort of intimidated them and they were a little afraid of her. These comments took me by surprise as I never felt that at all from her or perceived it from others. She was just as sweet as could be. If I had to guess,

I'd say her sometimes serious, stoic demeanor came from her growing up the oldest of seven children on a farm, with lots of responsibilities to attend to.

My mother was a homemaker, creating a wonderful environment for us. But she was so much more. She was also involved in lots of clubs and organizations in Dunkirk. One of them was the Women's Research Club in which members would investigate a topic or issue, write it up and present it to the group. She was also active in Eastern Star and was very active in the church, heading up chicken noodle dinners and other fundraising and social functions. She was also a member of the Republican Women, the election committee, the Dunkirk Alumni Association, and volunteered at the Minnetrista Center in Muncie. She received the Dunkirk High School alumni service award as she worked hard on keeping track of all the alumni and sending out invitations to the yearly get-together. Only recently did I review a scrapbook my sister lovingly put together of my mother's certificates and newspaper articles—and I saw my mom in a way I've never seen her or acknowledged her before. I was flabbergasted at the awards and statewide recognition she had received for her accomplishments. All at the same time I felt both intensely proud of her and a little ashamed at myself for never recognizing how amazing she was when I was growing up.

Then there was my father—a typical '60s dad from what I could tell. He was a hardworking man who kept food on the table and toys in the yard and provided a good home for his family. While my dad was a likeable and friendly man, I always wondered what it would have been if we'd been even closer when I was growing up—a little more like buddies who did even more stuff together. But we all played our societal roles consistently, and I have nothing but praise for this man who people knew simply as "Johnny."

My father was born in Muncie, but came to Dunkirk at age two when his parents decided to return here. I like to think of Dad as a little like "Spanky" McFarland from the "Our Gang" series, and ironically, they were born in the same year, 1928. He resembled Spanky with his dark features, round face, and more than generous girth. Spanky was also known to be a little mischievous and the leader to some of his minions, as was my father. He wore a stylish flat top for many years and administered just a dab of butch wax to ensure it keep its shape. Later in life he let his hair grow out and even when he passed away at age 78, still had a full, dark, thick head of hair—the kind that would make the ladies envious. The only dusting of gray hair on the man could be found residing discretely in the full, well-groomed mustache he sported for practically his whole adult life.

Dad was a tradesman; he went to carpet installation school in New York, then teamed with Grant Fager laying carpet for Stewart Brothers Furniture, Inc., serving the townspeople's need for many years. My father and Grant were both known to be jokesters around Dunkirk. One of the funniest things I recall is when they turned the windshield washer nozzle on their van to face outward. When they stopped at a traffic light in downtown Dunkirk, they'd wait for someone they knew to cross the street, then spray their unsuspecting victim as they passed—always good for a belly laugh and the potential for payback.

Our household was a bit like *Father Knows Best* or *The Donna Reed Show.* Two parents. Two kids. The father worked. The mother was a housewife. The two kids did stuff and were involved in activities at school and in the community. Our family kept to a regular schedule. Connie and I got up at about 7 a.m., had a quick breakfast of cereal or Pop Tarts or instant oatmeal, and took off to meet the bus for school or start our walk. Dad got up at about the same time, had breakfast, and was off to work at about 7:45.

Our evening supper schedule during the week was always structured. Mom had it ready at 5:30 p.m. and we would all converge in the kitchen where we had our assigned, or "regular," seats along the counter. Supper was always cooked by my mother in the kitchen and we never went out on weekdays because of school the next day. We would have very Midwestern meals like meat loaf and macaroni and cheese. Fried chicken and mashed potatoes. Roast with potatoes. Chicken and noodles or tuna salad.

After our meal, my father would get up and go into the living room or basement to his workshop. He would either fiddle in his workshop or sit in his Lazy Boy chair to watch TV and read the *Muncie Evening Press* and relax. My mother was responsible for all the cleanup. These "traditional" roles were most likely observed by millions of households in America during the '60s and never raised an eyebrow. The wife cooked, did the housework, and, basically, waited on everyone else in the house. Today this would be sexist, if not intolerable to most, but, quite simply, this is the way it was in the '60s. My father wasn't being disrespectful or difficult or lazy; he was fulfilling his expected household role and providing for our family in other ways. In his defense, he had worked all day at a purely physical job on his hands and knees laying carpet and linoleum, and he was tired, for sure. He and Grant carried giant rolls of carpet on their shoulders into customers' homes. They also had to carry carpeting from the store into their truck, and occasionally had to carry a roll of carpeting up the stairs into the carpet "cutting room," a second story room that contained a large carpet "sewing machine," remnants, and used furniture.

Dad took great pride in his hobby of wood crafting. His woodshop was quite impressive, containing about every electric tool you can think of, including a table saw, jig saw, lathe and drill press. He loved making things, as evidenced by the list of his creations, included a couple of tables that had inlaid checker or chess boards. A sailboat. Various and assorted wooden games. Picture frames. Book shelves. Wooden toys. He was very proud of what he made and would donate lots of wooden toys and games to the church to be sold at their annual bazaar. My sister and I would accompany him in his workshop, but he was a bit particular about the way he did things; in fact, he never really taught us how to use most of the electric tools. I'm not sure if it was a safety issue or whether he was more of a "doer" than a "teacher." Nevertheless, he was a talented wood worker and loved working with his hands.

Elementary School

DUNKIRK HAD THREE SCHOOLS IN the '60s. Sutton Elementary School, a building constructed in the '20s, which housed students in third through sixth grades. Westlawn Elementary School, which housed students in first, second, and some third grade, constructed in the early '60s, and Dunkirk High School, which housed students in grades seven through twelve. When I was in kindergarten, it was held in what was known as the Scout Cabin, a small unassuming cement block building on West Commerce Street. The building was very simple and had a 12-inch vinyl tiled floor, a small kitchenette in the back, and two small restrooms.

Kindergarten consisted of a morning class and an afternoon class. I sat at a small table with other young kids (sometimes, smelly kids), taking a nap on the mat each of us brought from home, using round tipped scissors to cut things out, and using paste to glue stuff together. I can remember other kids being together, but I don't recall forging any friendships with any of the other children. (Maybe I was smelly too and didn't know it.) We were like cats, I'm sure, and our kindergarten teacher tried to herd us daily.

I was one of the first students to attend the brand new West-lawn Elementary School as a first grader. The school was state of the art and had six classrooms, a large multipurpose room used for lunch and other activities, a kitchen, and two nice bathrooms. It also had a state of the art playground with swings, monkey bars, and a bunch of other devices adventurous young kids loved to use. In second grade I was a student in Miss Powell's room, a divided class containing both second and third graders and where, literally, the second graders were lined up on one side of the class and the third graders on the other. I still wonder why I was part of this class and often hope it was because they saw some potential in a young eight-year-old Greg. My grades were all A's and B's and my report card was marred only slightly by the occasional negative comment of needing improvement in citizenship (whatever that was), sometimes completing my work carelessly, or being in too much of a hurry.

In the third grade, it was time to move up to Sutton Elementary School, a three-story building constructed in the '20s located about 200 yards from Westlawn. I was in Mrs. Inman's class and it was 1963/1964, a school year in which a couple of significant events in U.S. history occurred. The first occurred on Friday, November 22, 1963. As we were sitting in Mrs. Inman's class, Steve Bell, a sixth grader, appeared in the door and announced, "The president has been shot." I don't recall having any reaction to his announcement and I'm sure we continued doing whatever we were doing. A short time later, Steve appeared at the door again and announced, "The president has died." The next few days are a blur, but I can remember watching Sunday's black and white television broadcast of the funeral procession of our fallen president John F. Kennedy, and how, just a year earlier, my family had visited Washington D.C. and how my parents joked with me about perhaps Carolyn Kennedy being a potential girlfriend for me. For those who were alive on this date, it's one of those "where were you when" events that you'll always remember.

The other significant U.S. event that happened in 1963 can simply be described as "The Beatles." Oh my, what an impact they had on us. I remember buying their forty-five, *I Want to Hold Your Hand* and standing around the record player in the living room listening to it with my sister and parents. Buying this forty-five led to the purchase of many more Beatles singles, and to this day, I still have them, complete with the original sleeves; hopefully, they're worth a mint! Back in the classroom, we had a talent activity coordinated by Mrs. Inman and we formed a lip sync band to simulate The Beatles. Once a week we'd set up our group in front of the class and lip sync to an actual Beatles record. I was Ringo, playing the drums my father made from fruit cans balanced on top of dowel rods.

Mrs. Fields' fifth grade class 1965 - 1966

Sixth grade brought about prestige, responsibility, and admiration. We were the "big men on campus" and were given tasks that gave us an edge of power over the less empowered first through fifth graders. One responsibility the sixth-grade boys had was to set up and tear down the lunch tables and chairs in the multipurpose room. We would compete with one another on how many folded metal chairs we could carry at once and relished the power and strength we had. I believe I could carry eight at a time. I was also given the responsibility of punching lunch tickets at the entrance to the cafeteria. This afforded me an opportunity to socialize with and get to know just about everyone in the school. A prestigious power job for a sixth grader. My grades continued to be all A's and B's and my behavior apparently had settled down as Mr. Guy Plymale, my sixth-grade teacher, commented that I had an exemplary interest in school work and an exemplary relationship of effort to ability. Mr. Plymale and our student teacher at the time, Mr. Keller, suggested I use my "exemplary" ratings, good grades and interest in physical activity and channel it into pursuing a career as an astronaut.

Sutton School had one distinguishing feature not seen in buildings of today and that was its tubular fire escape. Originating on the second-floor principal's office, the passageway was accessed through a door that led to a large tube that sloped downward to the ground. Each year we had a fire drill and for that one time only, we would be permitted into the principal's office, a large important-looking room containing a couple of massive wooden desks that was usually off-limits to all of us. We giddily lined up inside the office, waiting to slide down. One by one we descended through the darkness. This was not a smooth slide like you'd find at the playground; the joint where each section of the fire escape connected to the next was not smooth as the joints had begun to separate. But it was fun and it took time out of our regular studies, so we loved the fire drill and never really worried about an actual fire.

Sutton Elementary School

Music started to be integrated into the curriculum when we got a little older in fifth grade and Mr. Jon Dunning was the music teacher. He was a very personable guy, with short black hair and a subtle crooked smile, and the kids all loved him. Under his tutelage, our first introduction to playing an instrument was the flutophone, a lightweight plastic flute that was relatively easy to learn. We had music class in the basement music room where we sang beautiful, lilting songs. Mr. Dunning, I'm sure, wanted to improve the facilities to showcase our amazing talents as he surely recognized several who could potentially be stars. One day he got the idea that everyone should start bringing empty cardboard egg cartons so that we could glue them to the ceiling to create an acoustically beautiful music room. It was quite the cool thing to bring in your egg carton and get onto the ladder to glue it to the ceiling in front of your classmates, particularly the girls who were probably thinking about what an incredible stud you were for climbing the ladder. Unfortunately, Mr. Dunning didn't get permission to do this from the powers that be and the cartons were unceremoniously removed.

As elementary students, we were also exposed to other musical pursuits. I was thrilled when I got a guitar and started taking lessons at the Muncie Music Center, as I enjoyed envisioning myself the next John Lennon. My dad drove me to Muncie once a week for my lesson, which gave us some always welcomed "together" time. The small acoustically enclosed classrooms were in the basement and taught by a cool guy from Muncie who knew how to play chords. I, on the other hand, was awful. I repeat, AWFUL, and had trouble even understanding the concept of rhythm. Lessons didn't last too long, as I got frustrated and discovered that to be successful at something, it's probably a good idea to practice. My John Lennon visions began to dissolve. It did, however, give me the basis for playing the guitar in a group we formed in sixth grade. We called ourselves "The Nobles" with group members including Darrell McCowan on rhythm guitar, Paul Hart on organ, Scott Thompson on drums, Randy Miller as lead singer and lead banjo, and me on lead guitar. We had two "gigs"! One was at a sixth-grade event and the other was a private affair at the city park shelter house, the latter of which was a catastrophe in that we were scared to death and didn't play much of anything. I think we got paid a couple of bucks for showing up—or for leaving.

It's amazing how many songs you can play when you know three chords on the guitar. We rocked and rolled with our version of "Louis Louis," "House of the Rising Sun" and "Wild Thing." We would practice at Paul Hart's house due to his organ being located there. One day we discussed our group's name and whether we should change it from "The Nobles." My suggestion for an updated name was "Scott and his Tissues" (in honor of our drummer, Scott Thompson) but it was soundly rejected by the other group members. Perhaps my creative skills lie in other areas of music.

The Nobles

Elementary school was when most boys, I believe, start discovering that there are other kids in your class who, instead of just being pests, are kind of cute and for me this took place in the form of a "new" girl who just moved to town, Kristi Denny. She was different and intriguing and when I learned that she was born in the U.K., the same place the Beatles, Herman's Hermits, Peter and Gordon, and all the really cool musical groups of the mid '60s were from, well, I was smitten. Kristi and I went steady for a bit and I gave her a going steady ring—or rather, someone gave it to her for me. The funny thing about my relationship with Kristi is that I'm positive I never, ever, ever spoke to her face to face. Ever! What a Romeo!

Later in life I caught up to Kristi, who was living in Florida, via the magical social media platform called Facebook and we had great fun telling stories about our time in elementary and junior high school. One of the things I gleaned from seeing Kristi was that as you reflect with people you haven't seen in forty years, you discover there are many things you never knew about them when you were young. For example, I never understood the circumstances that brought Kristi to Dunkirk or couldn't even remember when she left, as I had moved on to other interests. As naive children, we're protected from certain life events, sometimes tragic, that impact families and I think this is a good thing. In today's world, I'm not certain the same amount of discretion still exists. I think it's okay to not expose young kids to all of life's challenges, tragedies, and disappointments. We could all use a little more innocence.

High School

IN 1967 DUNKIRK HIGH SCHOOL included students in grades 7-12 and we started off the year with 422 total students. My seventh-grade class had 78 students and the rumors of what happened to incoming seventh graders were running wild. Initiation! We were told that the seniors were particularly dangerous and that one of the initiation rituals involved picking up the seventh graders and setting them on a water fountain—better than setting them on fire I guess. Another rite of passage was placing them into the "pits" at the rear of the school, which were the access to the windows for the basement of the gymnasium, and good luck climbing out of them.

My first day of high school, we huddled at Mike Wise's house, located about one block from school, prior to making our entrance, because there's strength in numbers. Mike's house felt safe as this was where our cub scout den had met for several years with Mary Ann Wise and Betty Fulkerson, our den mothers. We congregated there and apprehensively began the too-short walk to school en masse on this sunny warm day in September. Our cautious looks and naive demeanors, I'm sure, were quite evident, but to our surprise, no one was captured. No surprise attacks. No one was terrorized. We'd made it past phase one, the walk to school. It was still very intimidating to walk the halls of the school full of other students, changing classrooms every fifty minutes, maneuvering the stairway to different floors where our classes were held. Potential confusion lurked around every corner. Even after we had been given a tour of the building earlier in the summer to explain that room numbers that started with a one were on the first floor, two on the second floor, etc., we still, I'm sure, walked around with that "deer in the head-lights" look.

Dunkirk High School

I remember the high school as if I'd been there yesterday. Dunkirk High School was a red brick building built sometime in the '20s and had two upper levels and one level partially un-derground. The floors were hardwood and varnished to a tee. They must have revarnished the floors every summer and I can still remember the distinctive smell. There were stairwells in the front and the back of the building. Most of the desks in the building were the more modern single seat with a small desktop attached, but at least two of the rooms, the study hall and the foreign language room, still had the old fashioned wooden desks that folded down from the desk behind it and contained an ink well. The fold-down desks were probably original to the school and had people's initials carved in them from the past 45 years of use. Many were of a darker color, made so from years and years of students' greasy fingers and ink covered papers.

Lockers lined the hallway leading to the library and the principal's office on the top floor, commonly known as "Suicide Hall"—named for the inevitable chaos that ensued between classes in this hallway and, I would speculate, to intimidate the underclassmen as the seniors and some juniors had their lockers there. The lockers on the bottom floor, near the home economics and chemistry rooms and bathrooms, were for seventh and eighth graders. There was a hierarchy of who got what locker and as you progressed in age, grade, and status, you got a better positioned locker. As a senior I had probably the best locker in the building, located at the entrance to Suicide Hall, where I would stand guard between classes, leaning suavely against the wall. When I graduated I "willed" the locker and the place I leaned on the wall to my friend and junior, Jeff Brown. We never had locks on our lockers and I never remember there being an issue with theft or destruction of property.

Suicide Hall, Dunkirk High School

Lunches at school were only 40-45 minutes, so you had to be efficient. Eating in the lunchroom, with your cronies at your favorite table, was just a precursor to spending free time. We quickly gobbled down the food on our trays with the separate little compartments and then could leave the school property. We frequently walked south on Main Street to Moon Man Martin's store to buy candy. Sometimes we'd just hang out in the front of the school building talking. During the winter, we headed to the gym and hung out in the bleachers. Sometimes we'd set up the volleyball nets and play barnyard volleyball, where you could let the ball hit the floor once. Usually we just sat in the bleachers and talked. One time I remember Jeff Ford and I getting our band instruments out, Jeff with saxophone and me with baritone horn, standing on the stage across from the assembled masses of students and playing a couple of songs.

The dress code in high school in the late '60s was pretty boring with boys wearing jeans and button-down collared shirts. The boys also wore what would now be considered dress shoes. Wing tips or loafers. Penny loafers were popular in the early '70s, aptly named because there was a slot in the top of the "slip-on" for a penny. Girls wore dresses—never pants. Only later in the early '70s do I remember girls being allowed to wear "culottes," a garment mildly resembling pants, having two legs, but looking more like a skirt. T-shirts were allowed but no writing on them was permitted even though the t-shirt fad was just beginning.

In junior high and high school, we were all required to take gym class. Everyone was required to buy and wear the green Dunkirk High School gym shorts and the white school-issue t-shirt. There was a place on each garment to write your name, so as not to get your uniform mixed up with others. We participated in all the requisite gym class activities and awkwardly took showers after each class in the dingy showers in the basement of the gymnasium.

In the '60s the baseball World Series was played during the day and I remember lining up and sitting in the basement hallway near gym teacher and coach Roy Sneed's office to listen to the game. I imagine the Reds were playing for the title and Coach was a big fan. I'm not sure how this qualified for P. E., but it was a nice relief from our normal gym activities.

In high school, almost everyone had a study hall and I industriously used my time there to do homework. In the given 55 minutes, I was usually able to complete almost everything.

I'd fix my eyes on the large clock on the wall in study hall and, as a senior, I would time the bell to the second — anticipating the bell's ringing, I'd stand up and walk toward the door with about three seconds before it sounded, always ensuring I was the first to leave the room. This worked every time and I never got into trouble, maybe because I was a senior.

The teachers at Dunkirk High School tended to be a mix of recent college graduates and veteran teachers. We were always told that Mrs. Harshman, an older lady with gray hair, glasses, and deceptively inviting smile, was a very demanding teacher but that it was worth the effort to persevere and take the dreaded senior literature class she taught — that it would pay off in the long term. Required reading in her class included such classics as *Animal Farm, 1984, Of Mice and Men, The Jungle,* and *Hamlet.* She was all business and, yes, she was tough and, yes, it did take much effort as not all of us in the class were brought up as book readers. But, they were right — her class helped us discipline ourselves and better prepare for the rigors of college.

My math teachers during my high school years included Mr. Harold Minnich, Mr. Frank Lovis, and Mr. Fred Smith. One of my favorites was Mr. Smith who taught senior trigonometry and linear algebra. All these teachers added value to my education and dedicated themselves to making sure we understood the basics of mathematic sciences. Mr. Smith was also a farmer and a no-nonsense teacher and regardless of his not taking much disobedience from us, which we dished out regularly, I still respected and liked him. As seniors, classmates Paul Hart, Rocky

Walker, Ron Louks and I would relentlessly goof off during his presentations and when his back was turned and he was writing on the board, we would shoot spit wads at each other using ink pens without their innards. One time a spit wad landed in the chalkboard tray just below where Mr. Smith was writing on the board, and I was shocked he didn't see it bouncing around in the tray—or he saw it and ignored it completely. Another time someone sent a spit wad in the direction of Rick Hornbaker and it landed directly on his forehead and stuck. Paul Hart and I were cracking up laughing as Mr. Smith had his back turned and didn't react at all. Cool as a cucumber.

I sometimes feel a little ashamed of all the goofing off we did in Mr. Smith's class as I liked and respected him and felt as though we took a little advantage of him. Later, I found out my father knew Mr. Smith on a personal basis and I think this made me feel guilty. Mr. Smith was by no means a pushover. A man of small stature, but obvious strength, which could be seen in his weathered leathery hands, he had coached basketball at Dunkirk High School early in his career, a job that required leadership and a demand for discipline from his student athletes.

Mr. Arthur Sellers, a young man in his thirties with short black hair and a bit of a rotund physique, taught chemistry and physics and was a very likable fellow who related well to us. Mr. Sellers drove an AMC Pacer of which he was very proud. My impression is that he wanted to be one of the guys as he seemed to get along nicely with the Dunkirk High School athletes. Mr. Sellers was a weight lifter and invited the track team to his garage in the spring to lift weights to improve our performances. I was skeptical of doing this as I feared it would negatively impact my performance in the sprint and high jump competition, but, regardless, we still visited his garage gymnasium and lifted. It turned out to be a good thing and I appreciated the interest Mr. Sellers took in our overall health and well-being.

We had the choice of taking either French or Latin at Dunkirk High School, and I opted for French, taught by Mrs. Novel, our foreign language teacher. A class requirement was to take on a new French name, so I selected Louis as mine, and we were required to speak French during the entire class. Interestingly, Mrs. Novel was born in Italy and spoke with an accent, and I'm sad to say I don't know her story as to why she came to the U.S. and ended up at Dunkirk High School. I know where she lived, just south of Dunkirk, along highway 67, at the top of a hill as one snowy day students were invited to come over and sled down her slope. Looking back and if she were alive today, I think Mrs. Novel would be a fascinating person to get to know.

Mr. Fred Beeson was perhaps the most popular high school teacher to ever grace the halls at Dunkirk. A jovial, youthful man with a high energy level, he almost seemed larger than life with his big personality and his no-nonsense persona. He was a man who both demanded your respect and was also a person you wanted to be around. Mr. Beeson taught history, sociology, speech and drivers training. In the summer before our sophomore year we took drivers training and Mr. Beeson was our instructor. We had two cars, one donated by Fuqua Chrysler Plymouth and one donated by Crown City Chevrolet. With Mr. Beeson at the helm, in my car were fellow classmates Marvin Buckner, Rocky Walker, and Paul Hart, all good friends of mine. Mr. Beeson was very specific and stern teaching us the rules of the road, but he was also good natured and playful. He took us out one day in his personal car, which had a three-speed manual on the column, and instructed us on how to drive a stick. At the end of the course, Marvin, Rocky, Paul, and I showered Mr. Beeson with Tiparillo Cigars as a thank you for being our teacher, knowing that he liked to occasionally puff on one.

Don and Lois Casterline were also teachers at the school. Mr. Casterline, who was probably in his fifties and was pretty much all business, taught shop and my father always had good things to say about him as he had been my dad's teacher, too. Later I learned that my father got all A's in shop, so I understand why he liked Mr. Casterline so well. His grades were either a testament to my dad's skill at making things, or an indication as to where his interests lay. Back in those days, all male students were required to take shop, while girls were required to take home economics taught by Martha Kegerreis. For shop, we all built the required "pump lamp" to pass the course. We concentrated on shop safety and how basic tools worked. We also had the opportunity to make something to our own liking, and so I decided to build a wooden box to safely store my valuables. Mrs. Casterline, Mr. Casterline's wife taught English and tried her best at instructing us on the use of proper grammar and sentence structure. She was a teacher who was serious about her job and I think didn't understand that students needed a bit of levity and laughter during classroom activities. This didn't particularly translate to popularity, but did translate well to learning and I benefitted greatly from her efforts.

Then there was our music instructor, Mr. Tom Grzesik, a relatively thin man of average height and short dark hair who was fresh out of college. He directed the marching, concert and pep bands. I always thought Mr. Grzesik was "misunderstood" as a teacher and students tended to not relate to him well. He was very focused and didn't mess around-- and I think that type of personality is a requirement for teachers who are trying to mold young musicians into a cohesive unit that sounds respectable. I always liked Mr. Grzesik and he always treated me with respect. Under his leadership, I learned to play the cornet—a shorter version of the trumpet—but later converted to playing the baritone horn in the marching and concert bands.

Mr. Weldon LeMaster, a well-liked teacher, taught history and geography and was our "class sponsor," which means he oversaw our responsibility of planning and creating the junior/senior prom and was the main chaperone on our senior trip. Then there was Mr. J. Forrest Luker, our beloved school counselor. Mr. Virgal Kesler, our principal. Mr. Terry Cheek, a very popular history and English teacher. Mr. Tom Jerles, a tall, outgoing teacher from nearby Albany who always had a smile on his face and who would eventually be the successful assistant basketball coach. And Mr. Bob Phillips, a Dunkirk native who was just a few years older than us and so could relate to the students very well. Mr. Phillips headed up the school newspaper, *The Blotter*, and oversaw the yearly junior and senior plays.

Every teacher I had in elementary, junior high, and high school—even several I didn't have in the classroom—had a positive impact on my life. It's almost unbelievable, as if something out of a storybook, and I am inclined to feel I hit the proverbial jackpot, at least where teachers were concerned. Some were more impactful than others, sure, but when you hear people give credit to teachers and say that they were responsible for developing you as a person, it is true. Teachers are probably one of the most underrated and under-appreciated group of people, and in today's world of additional challenges confronted by teachers (misbehavior, substance abuse, potential violence), they have an even more difficult job. I always respected my teachers and even today, at over sixty years old, I have a difficult time not referring to or greeting an old teacher by Mr. or Mrs. or Coach. They all still hold a special place in my heart and I can't talk about any of them without feeling that admiration and respect I still have for them.

I lived about one mile from school and in earlier years rode the bus. Even though, technically, we lived in town, the bus would stop at the end of our driveway. Mr. Everett Gordon, a local farmer, was my bus driver and every Christmas he would give each student a small sack of candies, most of which were hard candies. After I got on the bus, we still had a few stops out in the country southeast of Dunkirk. Mr. Gordon was a very kind man and I don't ever remember there being behavioral issues on the bus, such the kind as you hear about frequently these days.

As I got older, it became uncool to ride the bus so I would maintain my cool status by walking the mile to school. Sometimes it was cold and sometimes snowy and slick. I got good at walking on ice and compacted snow while carrying a gym bag and books and cannot remember ever slipping or falling. Other days I would ride in with my friend Paul Hart who lived about three blocks from me and had a 1964 four door Chevy Impala. As a junior or senior, I would walk the three blocks to his house and wait until he was ready to go and then we would drive to school together.

My trip home after school was usually late and dark because of after-school basketball practice, but I had worked out a system with my parents whereby I would go to the pay phone booth located at the corner next to the school and call home and let it ring one time. They would then call the phone booth back to verify that it was me and in that way, I would avoid having to put money in the phone. Waiting for my parents to pick me up, or during the times I walked home, I remember my hair, which was still wet from my shower after practice, freezing like a helmet. A very cold helmet.

When we graduated in 1973, our seventh-grade class had dwindled from 78 students to a graduation class of 49 students. This number includes four students who had moved into town during junior high or high school, and it means we lost 33 students between seventh and twelfth year. Where did they go? I know several had been reassigned to either Albany High School or Blackford High School as they lived in Delaware County or Blackford County, and Dunkirk sat precariously at the corner of and overlapped those counties. So it was decided to send those students elsewhere. But, I look back and wonder what happened to all the students who just sort of disappeared… Did they drop out, or move away, or attend special schools?

Sports: Little League, Basketball, Cross Country, Track

The 1961 Dunkirk High School sectional champs

SPORTS PLAYED A BIG PART of my life in the '60s and early '70s. Living in a neighborhood of several boys about the same age, we played much basketball and baseball, which led to the normal progression of being a part of organized sports, and this started with Little League baseball.

Dunkirk had a thriving Little League program, and being on a team was a normal thing for everyone. Every boy had his own baseball mitt, most likely purchased at the local Watson's sporting goods store. All we needed was to be chosen for a team, given a uniform donated by a local business, and carted off to the baseball diamond for some organized practice. I was a member of the Manifold Farms team for a couple of years. We played during the week and diligently followed the instructions of the local volunteer coaches, usually one who had a son on the team. The most important player on the team was usually the pitcher, with all other team members being assigned other positions the coach thought we could play.

In that snazzy Little League outfit

We played at the Dunkirk City Park, a large park that contained a shelter house, full basketball court, several pieces of playground equipment, and acres and acres of grassy areas for picnics. The baseball diamond was typical of the times and included a dirt infield, two cement block constructed dugouts, and two small bleacher areas for adoring fans and family members. Behind the backstop was probably the most important characteristic of the baseball field and that was the concession stand because, to us, the most important part of the game was afterward—when the coach would line us up for our treat, regardless if we won or lost.

Progressing into junior high school gave us more opportunity for organized sports with track and field, and the king of all Indiana sports: basketball.

I started playing organized basketball in the seventh grade, and we had a gaggle of young boys who came out for the team. Anyone who could walk and chew gum was eligible, and I'm sure for the coach it was like trying to corral a bunch of puppies dribbling and shooting basketballs. Our practices had to be juggled with the practices of the varsity team because we only had one gymnasium for grades seven through twelve, which meant we sometimes practiced early morning before school. Junior high school basketball was an experience that prepared us fundamentally for the future as we would do countless drills, get used to playing against other good players, and become comfortable playing in front of crowds. As junior high players, we attended all the high school games and marveled at how big and how good the varsity players were.

Seventh grade basketball team 1967 - 1968

The seventh and eighth-grade coach in 1967-68 was Mr. Dwight Michael. Back then I thought he was mean and yelled a lot—most likely because we weren't used to being coached and being told what to do. We were a rag tag bunch of skinny and awkward young future star athletes and would participate in drills and scrimmages. One of our players, Scott Thompson, was already almost six feet tall and had a bright future as a center. Some others on the team, quite frankly, were not athletes and were probably encouraged by their parents to join the team because in Indiana, hey, that's what you do. I had benefitted from playing ball with my buddies from the neighborhood for years prior to having an organized team and in 1967-1968 there was no such thing as youth, club or pee wee basketball in Dunkirk.

My freshman year in 1969-1970, the coaches at Dunkirk were varsity coach Jim Hammel (who went on to coach an Indiana state runner-up team in 1991-1992 at Lafayette Jeff High School and then the Indiana High School all-stars in 1993) and B-team coach Roy Sneed. Coach Hammel grew up in Huntington and was an outstanding athlete there. He attended Ball State, located about 15 miles from Dunkirk. Coach Sneed was a Muncie Central graduate and hurdler on the track team there. He also graduated from Ball State. I remember both being introduced to the student body in 1967 as the new coaches of basketball, which was a big deal. They received an excited reception after several years of mediocre records by the Speedcats in the mid '60s.

I respected Coach Hammel; he had a zero-tolerance policy for misbehavior and published a list of training rules in 1969 that all players were to follow:

> Cleanliness of mind and body is the first secret of building a great team. No team can be a winner that does not observe the rules of clean living. The world loves a winner, but we all want victory with honor.
>
> It is well that each of us understand what is expected in the way of habits, diet, sleep, care of the body, and conduct on and off the court. No player should report for practice unless he is willing to obey these instructions and sacrifices that are advisable and necessary if he is to be in the best possible physical condition.
>
> The player who thinks that he can slyly break the training regulations, smoke an occasional cigarette, or keep late hours has the wrong idea. Please, if this is the way you feel, do not even bother trying out for our team. You will just be wasting both your time and mine. You will be almost sure to give yourself away sooner or later and you will not only be vio-

lating the trust placed in you, but you will be doing yourself, the school, and most of all your teammates a great injustice.

The training policies listed below were set up on August 19, 1969 at a joint meeting of our coaches and returning lettermen. Since these rules were made by the leaders of our program, we will both expect and demand that they be followed! Let's be fair with each other and not try to "beat" the rules.

I. Avoid the following practices and habits: smoking, gambling, drinking of alcoholic beverages, drinking of Cokes, Pepsi, etc. (if you want a soft drink, make it a 7-Up, Sprite, or Teem), pastries, misconduct—on and off the court, roughhousing in showers, etc., irregular attendance, classroom ineligibility, tardiness to practice—be on the floor within ten minutes after the final bell, worry—it saps your interest and vitality. If you have a problem, come in and we will talk it over in private.

II. Hours: Weekdays (Sun - Thurs) - home by 9:00; in bed by 10:00. Night before games: home by 8:00; in bed by 9:00. Weekends (no game the following day): home by 12:00; in bed by 12:30. After away or home games (game the next night): straight home and to bed.

III. Dates: No dates on weekdays (Sun - Thurs). No dates the night before a game.

IV. Driving: No riding with anyone of school age

(high school or college). If you must drive in case of an emergency, contact Coach Hammel as soon as possible!

V. Hats: Hats will be worn at all times when outdoors.

VI. Hair: Length of hair and sideburns will be determined individually by the coaching staff. Razor cuts are not allowed.

VII. Meals: Eat three regular, hearty meals a day. Don't overeat!

VIII. Conduct with Girls: It has been agreed that there will be no physical contact of any kind with girls on the school grounds, downtown area, or any other public place. We feel that this is a must if you are to gain the respect and desire as ATHLETES.

Coach Hammel also coached my freshman team and established a C team, which consisted of freshmen and sophomores. The C team gave sophomores an opportunity to see a little more playing time rather than sit on the bench during B-team games.

My sophomore year, B-team coach Sneed took over the C-team duties. I was on the roster of both the B and C teams and saw playing time primarily on the C team. Our B team was stacked with talent and we had several freshmen who got a lot of playing time. Mark Hoagland, Cliff Dunnington and Jeff Brown were the freshman who played B-team ball and were destined to be big contributors to future varsity teams.

As a junior I played on the B team and "dressed" for the varsity team. I was the only junior on the B team and my teammates were mostly sophomores, with a few freshmen, including Craig Fulkerson, Bobby Davenport and Rodney Rouch. I played every B-team game during the 1971-1972 season and almost every minute of every game, averaging just under 10 points a game with two games of 18. I dreamed of having a game of 20 points, but it never quite happened. I led the team in offensive rebounds, a testament to my hustle and scrappiness, something that probably extended my high school basketball playing career. I think I also lead the team in turnovers. I was listed as at 5' 10" and played forward because my ball handling skills were a bit sketchy. I laughingly referred to myself as a "jumping jack" forward.

Dunkirk High School B-team 1971 - 1972

As a junior I dressed for the sectional game at Blackford High School, and Jim Hammel was the varsity coach. Coach Hammel's brother was Bob Hammel, the sports writer for the Bloomington newspaper and so covered Indiana University sports and knew the coaches. After our sectional loss, a very tall man came into our locker room and spoke to us for a couple of minutes. It seems the tall guy was there scouting a high-scoring, hotshot player from Bryant High School named Tom Weigel, for Indiana University. The tall guy was the infamous Bobby Knight and it was his second year as head coach at IU; I had no idea who he was until later.

Official Varsity portrait 1971 - 1972

Entering my senior year of high school, I knew that every player from the prior year's varsity basketball was returning. Varsity Coach Jim Hammel left to take on a new opportunity, I believe, at Austin High School and my B-team coach, Roy Sneed, was given the opportunity to be a varsity high school basketball coach.

Being a B-team player the prior year, I had much anxiety about whether I would make the varsity as a senior. I would be, maybe, the twelfth player, and was concerned that Coach Sneed might not want a senior on the team in that spot. I remember lying in bed thinking about what it might take to make the team. I wrote out a list of the players and tried to figure out who would be on the team and where I stood. I would review the list over and over, and determined that junior Jeff Harker and I would be vying for the eleventh and twelfth positions on the team. Finally, the day came when the typed list of players making the roster was posted on the coach's door. I nervously walked down the stairs to the coach's office. My eyes anxiously scanned the list of names... and. there it was, like spotting a coveted Christmas present under the tree: Greg Retter. I had made the varsity team!

Playing on a high school varsity basketball team in Indiana is as good as it sounds—one of the most memorable and gratifying experiences of my life. If ever there was a pinnacle of growing up Hoosier, this was it. I'll never forget that year on the varsity team and I'm thankful for the amazing and cool experiences it gave me.

In today's world of Indiana high school basketball, Dunkirk High School would be considered a Single A team consisting of the smallest schools as we had about 250 students in grades 9-12. We played smaller schools in east central Indiana and in the '60s and '70s there were plenty to choose from. High school consolidations were in their infancy then and Jay County had five schools (Dunkirk, Pennville, Bryant, Redkey, and Portland). We would occasionally venture into the "bigger" school category and play Norwell, Blackford, Union City, South Adams, schools that had, in some cases, already consolidated and who had state of the art gymnasiums, meaning they had bleachers that actually folded.

Dunkirk Speedcat basketball was the big game in town and on Friday nights and sometime Saturday nights, it's what everyone did—go to the game. We'd arrive in our Speedcat blazers, shirt and tie and sit together on the bench, across from most of the crowd situated in the permanent wooden bleachers. We spectated from a bench during the B-team game and then at the start of the last quarter we'd go to the locker room and get dressed for the game. Coach Sneed would come down and give us instructions on our game plan, discuss some of the competitor's strengths and weaknesses, and generally give us a pep talk. When the time came, we would file through the hallways of the basement locker room and ascend the steps into the gymnasium.

B-team huddle with the Varsity waiting in the background 1972 - 1973

Then finally, that one special moment arrived when we would run out onto the gymnasium floor to the cheering throngs of crazed fans. It was electric! Wearing our long warmup pants and our short sleeve warmup tops with our last name snapped onto the back, we couldn't have been more proud. After a few minutes, we'd remove our long pants, exposing our snug fitting game shorts and our high-top socks pulled up to our knees, which consisted of green striped stirrup socks covered by long white tube socks. Beneath the warmup tops, we wore a short sleeve synthetic top with a big D on the front and our names embroidered on the back. Our shoe options expanded my senior year with either the usual white high top Converse All-Stars or the new choice, green low top Converse All-Stars.

Warm-up was a way not only of warming up our bodies but also getting used to the crowd. For me, this was nerve wracking. With B-team play the year before, crowds weren't very big, but the varsity is what everyone came to see. Even in the comfort of the Dunkirk High School gym where I'd practiced for hours on end, it was still a bit intimidating to be in front of a packed house. I remember spotting my mother and father sitting in the bleachers about ten rows up. They had season tickets and would always buy an extra seat to put their coats on. My uncle Gary also attended several games, sitting in my parents' extra seat. I was aware they were there, but was more focused on the task at hand—warming up, going through our pre-game drills, and getting a glance at the opponents.

I tell people I once scored 24 points…in the warmups. Unfortunately, I didn't play much my senior year, as we had too many other good players. Around Christmastime we held the annual Big 4 tournament, which consisted of teams from Redkey, Pennville, Albany and Dunkirk. My senior year we were the favorites and I had dreams of cutting the nets down after a big tourney win, something I had never had the opportunity to do. Unfortunately, we got ousted in the first game of the tourney and I was very upset because I didn't feel my team had played as hard as it should have. Even though I didn't play in that game, that loss was tough to take, as I desperately wanted to cut down the nets after a tourney win.

Dunkirk High School Varsity 1972 - 1973

Our sectional basketball tourney was held at Blackford High School. Blackford had a new, large, well-lit gymnasium. Built a couple of years prior, it had bleachers that folded up, a light colored natural wood floor, a sweet sound system, modern locker rooms, a full-sized playing floor, and the best feature of all, a place where our names were displayed on the wall.

In 1973, Indiana had a single class basketball tourney, which meant that sectionals were established based on geography and not on school size. Sectionals generally were hosted by a school with the biggest gymnasium in the area and Blackford was the one. Success in the tourney was based on progressing in the tourney because only one school in the state could be crowned state champion. Success at Dunkirk High School had been minimal the past few years and townspeople still remembered the team that made it to the Regional final game in 1959. For us and for many schools, success might be to play in the Sectional final game, or just to win a game, as excitement built the further in the tourney you progressed. Unfortunately, our season ended quickly as we were beaten by Blackford in our first game of the sectional.

Our loss in the Blackford sectional still stings. As I walked off the floor I realized it would be the last time I'd wear basketball Speedcat green and white. Fortunately, it was March and that meant track season would begin soon and, in fact, we had an indoor track meet scheduled at South Adams High School for the Tuesday following our Sectional loss—a reason to go on.

Overall, we'd had a good season my senior year in 1973; heck, we ended up going 14-6. And I was fortunate to have started one game, on Senior Night. I played in a few games, averaging 2 points per game, but mostly got mop up playing time. Still, being part of Indiana high school basketball was indubitably one of the coolest things I've ever done.

At Dunkirk High School, we started our basketball season early, in late October. In fact, we were one of the first schools to play in the state. This was primarily because we didn't have a football team and at most schools in the '60s and '70s, several athletes played both football and basketball. As basketball players, we were required to participate in one of two activities prior to trying out for and practicing for basketball. One was cross country, which most players chose, as did Paul Hart, Marvin Buckner and I. Scott Thompson and Chip Phillips opted for the dreaded, unimaginable, horrible "conditioning program," which mostly no one wanted to participate in but those who enjoyed pain. The program consisted of workouts in the gym, running ladders, running bleacher laps and an assortment of other masochistically concocted workouts. It was late August and the gym's only source of coolness was when we opened the large windows near the top of the gym behind the permanent bleachers.

Dunkirk High School cross country team 1972 - 1973

In cross-country, our coach was Roy Sneed and one of his sayings included something like, "Training doesn't really start until you're tired," which meant we ran a lot. The camaraderie we had with teammates was nice and the environment quite enjoyable. We raced through nicely landscaped parks and golf courses and we trained by running around the streets of town. We did a three-mile loop that proceeded north of town on State Road 167, then cut to the east on County Road 300 South, then back to the south on County Road 1150 West. This three-mile loop was the longest continuous run I ever did in high school but it more than prepared us for the rigors of competitions. Sometimes, I will admit, we didn't run the whole way around the entire loop, as various and assorted types of "monkey business" waylaid us. One time we got the bright idea of cutting through the middle of the loop, which meant running through recently harvested soybean and corn fields and climbing over a few fences. Little did we know that cutting the course actually resulted in us probably getting a better workout than if we'd run the loop.

Another time we played a game of cross-country "hide and seek." The team was split into two groups. One group ran off into town and the other group was supposed to run into town and find them. In theory, this sounds like a fun thing to do and a bit more interesting than just running around in circles. Unfortunately, Coach Sneed didn't anticipate our creativity, as our group decided to hide in a barn for the duration of the workout about two blocks from the school near where Bob Mayo lived. I'm sure Paul Hart was the mastermind in concocting our running group's strategy of not being found.

In 1971 Indiana high school cross-country consisted of a two-mile run, and in 1972 they upped it to a two-and-a-half-mile run. Our course was at the Dunkirk City Park where we would run two loops around its perimeter, with one segment circling a small roundabout and the shelter house. Just before the shelter house there was a cable about two feet high that we would have to hurdle. The rest of the course was on grass, crossing park roads about four times per loop. It was flat and fast, and we would run primarily dual meets with local small high schools.

Varsity cross country team relaxing before a meet

Cross-county courses in the early '70s took a variety of forms. At Delta High School, they were building a new school and behind it was some woods in which a swath was cut for a cross-country course. At Blackford High School, another new school, the course weaved its way behind the school through some similar woods.

As seniors, Rick Hornbaker and I rotated between being the sixth and seventh runner on the varsity. These were the non-scoring positions on a cross-country team as scores were determined by the first five runners. Only in the case of a tie were the sixth and seventh runners' finish position used. Blackford High, a school a bit larger than Dunkirk, had a good running program. One meet Rick and I were running together, bringing up the rear, when we approached a place you could cut the course. We were back in the woods where no spectators or coaches or other runners could see us. Without saying a word, Rick looked at me, I looked at him and, thinking we were so sly, we both cut the course—only to finish something like thirteenth and fourteenth.

After basketball season and in the spring, it was time to gear up for track. Our high school track was a quarter mile around and had a couple of unusual characteristics. It had a 220-yard straightaway and it was made of crushed limestone. Most tracks in the late '60s and early '70s were made of cinder, with the bigger schools having tracks made of tartan material. It was always a cool thing to run on a tartan track. Blackford and Union high schools both had tartan tracks. In Jay County, there were five high schools in the late '60s. Redkey, Pennville and Bryant high schools all had track teams, but none of them had a track. I've always wondered where and how they trained as all these schools had some good track and field athletes over the years. Portland, the largest school in the county, had a cinder track.

High jumping was my forté in track and field, and it all started in junior high when a few of us decided to take a bamboo pole down to the high school to practice jumping. We had become intrigued by watching Dick Fosbury in the 1968 Olympics utilize a new method of jumping that consisted of jumping over the bar backwards instead of the more traditional "western roll" or "scissors" techniques. Fosbury went on to win a Gold Medal in the Mexico City Olympics, and with this, a revolution in high jumping began. His technique (others were using it, but he was the one who received widespread coverage) became known as the "Fosbury Flop" when a local newspaper ran a photo and captioned it "Fosbury Flops Over Bar." The advent of using foam rubber landing services (instead of sawdust or sand) allowed this technique to gain widespread popularity.

We used the high-jump standards and foam landing pit at the high school, which remained outside at all times, located inside the track and having a grass takeoff point. We high-jumped a lot and the result was that we got proficient as it is a combination of timing and vertical leap and a bit of strength and speed. Through practice I developed good form and I already had a decent vertical leap.

In high school, track started after the last basketball game in March and it was still cold outside. We began our training inside the gymnasium and would either run circles around the basketball court or traverse a course around the court, up to the top of the bleachers, across the top of the bleachers, down the bleachers, across the court, up the stairs, across the stage and back down to the basketball court. This was a bit monotonous. The high jump pit was set up on the stage for practice, and our shot-putters used an "indoor friendly" shotput that wouldn't damage the basketball floor.

As weather conditions got better we were thrilled to be outside again and would happily run sprints and tempo runs on a course around the high school on the sidewalk. We would also run sprints diagonally on the school parking lot wearing our green cotton sweat pants and hooded sweat shirts. Once the track dried out and weather conditions improved, we started training on the crushed limestone track.

Our school was always fortunate to have plenty of guys who wanted to run track, and we had lots of guys who didn't participate in any other sport. I'm not sure what attracted so many to track and field. I'd like to think it was because we had so much fun, or maybe because there were so many opportunities for guys to compete. It might also have been because of Coach Roy Sneed. Coach had a blend of no-nonsense coaching, playfulness and relatability. Coach was only in his twenties and still participated in some of our sprint workouts, challenging us to beat him. He still had the stuff and could beat almost all of us in the forty-yard dash repeats we did on the school parking log. Coach also had a good knowledge of hurdling and helped develop Jeff Brown, our local track star, into a state champion threat in both the high and low hurdles.

Initially, I ran the 100-yard dash, 220-yard dash, 880-yard relay and high jumped. Our team was loaded with sprinters. Chip Phillips, Kim Younkin, Jeff Luzadder, Jeff Brown and Randy Sherman were all fast and so Coach Sneed had lots of options on who would run the 100 and 220.

The luxury of having so many sprinters was that the 880-yard relay was loaded with fast guys. My sprinter friends were a bit faster than I was, particularly in the 100, and Coach Sneed told me one day, "Retter, you're in the low hurdles." And so started my career running the low hurdles. Having some speed but less than graceful form, I was competitive but guaranteed to never win a race as Jeff Brown was a sure bet to obliterate all his competitors. As a senior, however, I was lucky enough to place in every low hurdle race, either second or third in dual meets and sometimes fourth in three-way meets. Jeff went undefeated.

Having so many sprinters on the team allowed us to have decent success in these events and the sprinting quartet of Kim Younkin, Chip Phillps, Jeff Brown, and myself went on to set relay records in the 880-yard relay (broken the year after I graduated) and the sprint medley relay (we still hold this record to this day).

As a high jumper, I continued to get stronger and better as I got older. I broke the school record in 1973 as a senior while competing at a meet at Wes Del High School. Competition was fierce and Wes Del had a good jumper. There was a bit of a crowd surrounding the parking lot where we were jumping and I assume the students at Wes Del knew that their jumper had some competition. The Wes Del jumper and I matched jumps and I made it over 6' 2", at which time I asked the official for a measurement as I knew this was a Dunkirk school record. Unfortunately, the measurement came up at 5' 11½" because of the bow in the bar, but still good enough for a record. Ironically, I got only second in the meet as the guy from Wes Del jumped 6' 4".

High jumping the "Fosbury Flop"

Our track team won two Jay County crowns the last two years I was in school and it was cool having success in that sport. Jeff Brown, our local track star, could run in just about any event and win. Jeff went on to finish an amazing third in the low hurdles and fifth in the high hurdles and was named Robert S. Hinshaw mental attitude winner in the Indiana High School state meet the year after I graduated. Jeff went on to Purdue where he ran track and was an All Big Ten performer. To this day, people in Dunkirk are proud of what Jeff accomplished, representing Dunkirk back in 1974.

1973 County track champions

Competing in track and field and playing Indiana high school basketball were two of the best experiences of my life, and my parents were always supportive of what I did. They showed up at just about every home track meet, my father after ducking out of work about an hour early. I often wondered what they thought of us high school boys who were running around in circles on the track in sometimes windy, rainy, chilly weather. They were probably just happy we had something good to be a part of.

During track season, Dunkirk High School held its annual "senior trip," which required that I miss a meet. The trip would last seven days and our class, sponsors (Mr. LeMaster, principal Virgil Kesler), and a few chaperones took buses to Pittsburgh, Gettysburg, Washington D.C., New York City and Philadelphia. I'm not sure what the objective of the trip was, other than sort of a "coming of age" and educational experience. It was a tradition for all classes to do this and it was, I'm sure, the first time some of my classmates had visited some of these places and for some, first time being outside of Indiana. My room-mates—Rocky Walker, Paul Hart and Marvin Buckner—and I had a pretty tame experience apart from some minor hijinks. Washington, D.C., was the most interesting place; we visited the Lincoln Memorial, Arlington Cemetery, Washington Monument and the Capital Building. Everyone got dressed up—boys wore suits and ties—for the group picture in front of the Capital Building. In New York City, we had "free time" and I remember as I wandered the streets of Manhattan, my perception was that everyone seemed to be in a big hurry to go somewhere. We also took a boat trip around Manhattan and I proudly recall the tour director complimenting the students from Indiana on being so well-behaved—a testament to our parents and the teachers who shaped our young lives.

Church

I ATTENDED MT TABOR UNITED Methodist Church on Pleasant Street as a youth, just as my father John and his father Roy had done. Mt Tabor was one of the older churches in town, built in 1891, and many of the local business people attended there. Originally just called the Methodist Church, it was renamed to Mt Tabor in the late '60s when the Methodist and EUB (Evangelical United Brethren) churches merged to become the United Methodist Church.

The main sanctuary at Mt Tabor seated about 200 and I remember one service, probably Easter, back in the late '60s or early '70s when we had a packed house. The classrooms on each side of the sanctuary, usually closed off by sliding doors, were opened and set up with folding chairs for the overflow. The attendance that day approached 300.

We attended Vacation Bible School in the summer and I still remember the smell of the paper sack lunches each person brought for the day. Outdoor activities such as eating our lunches, tag, and ring around the rosy were conducted in the soft, grassy area behind the church while more academic and spiritual related exercises were held inside. John Moore was the minister during the late '60s at Mt Tabor, and everyone loved him. He had a great sense of humor, particularly as it related to his being a bit height challenged as he always stood on a box behind the pulpit when he preached.

The Methodist church follows a process of appointing ministers such that they only stay a few years in each place, usually four to six years, and then they are transferred to a different church within the district. When Reverend Moore left, Stan Tobias was appointed. Reverend Tobias was a tall, outgoing man who oozed of kindness, compassion and humility. He always had a smile on his face and something positive to say. I tell people today that if they could meet Stan and not know he was a minister, they'd realize immediately he was special and would most likely think to themselves, *There is something about him that sets him apart.* I always felt Stan set the standard for what acting like a Christian would be. I remember my father commenting when Stan first came to town that he thought he was going to be "all right" because he had already stopped by the barber shop and blended right in with the locals. Unfortunately, both Reverend Tobias and his wife Doris both passed away from cancer at an early age.

For a brief time when I was just a youngster, one of my Sunday school teachers was a guy named Tony Meier. Tony taught from a predetermined curriculum and may have just been a replacement for our normal teacher. One class, he mentioned sort of casually that he had discovered religion while sitting in a foxhole in Europe several years earlier. It didn't really mean much to me at the time until years later when I learned that Tony was a World War II veteran who was involved in the Normandy D-day invasion and landed on Utah beach. Here was a man who seemed ordinary enough but who dutifully took an active part in his community around Dunkirk, making sure things operated smoothly. My admiration for Tony later in life couldn't have been greater.

The choir at Mt Tabor United Methodist Church sat behind the minister on pews set at a 45-degree angle to the congregation. Jeff Ford, Rock Fuqua, Mark Hoagland and I joined the adult chancel choir while still in high school and enjoyed singing with the more experienced adults. Of course, the minister was always the best singer and his wife the pianist. Pastor Tobias was a particularly good singer and his wife Doris played the piano. Our songs were easy and we didn't have men singing tenor and bass parts, only the melody of hymns.

At one time in our history, the choir would conduct processions from behind the church down the middle aisle behind the acolytes (usually two youngsters who wore white robes) who were to light the candles. The choir wore beautiful black and purple robes and it was quite the regal event. Later we discontinued marching and simply walked in from one side of the choir loft, behind the minister. One time, I was the first person to enter the choir loft, leading all the others. After I had gotten about half way into the pew and in front of the entire congregation, I looked around and Jeff Ford was standing in the doorway laughing. He had paused before entering the choir loft and let me walk into the church, in front of the congregation completely on my own.

Mt Tabor United Methodist Church

Frequently after church on Sunday mornings, we drove to Portland to eat at Richards Restaurant or drive the 40 miles north to the Kentucky Fried Chicken restaurant in Fort Wayne for lunch. My father was never in a big hurry and we would often take his "short cuts," which inevitably resulted in taking longer to return home. I enjoyed the lunches with family and the food, particularly the salad bars, but grew impatient on our slow return home as I had important things to do, like watching TV or going somewhere to play basketball.

Mt Tabor United Methodist was, and still is, a beautiful place. The pipe organ in the front of the sanctuary was disconnected many years ago, but the regal pipes remain. Its beautiful wood altar and podium are as they have always been, leaving a sacred legacy. The giant carved wood door leading into the church, still a thing of wonder, and the large bell, though no longer used, still hangs in the belfry, a reminder of its watch over the town of Dunkirk.

Downtown Dunkirk

ONE OF THE THINGS THAT differentiates small towns in the '60s and early '70s with those of today is the proliferation of small businesses. Dunkirk had just about everything you needed back in the day: a lumberyard, two hardware stores, two groceries, a furniture store, two drug stores, etc. Not only are a lot of these businesses now gone, but who owned businesses has also drastically changed. In the '60s, Wilson's shoe store was owned and operated by Mr. Wilson. Shoemaker's drug store was owned and operated by Mr. Shoemaker, the pharmacist. Stewart Brothers Furniture store was owned and operated by Bob and Don Stewart. Hubbard's hardware store was owned and operated by Mr. Hubbard. Today, retail businesses are typically owned by larger entities and run by employees, frequently of high schooler age, or older people working part time to make ends meet.

Downtown Dunkirk

When I was a kid Dunkirk had a "five and ten cent store" called Danners, part of a small chain in Indiana. One of the Danner family sons actually worked in the Dunkirk store for a while in the '70s. The store was a typical "dime store" oriented establishment and had a little of everything, to our great delight! Several rows were dedicated to towels and other home goods. They offered a variety of school supplies, including boxes of crayons, pencils, three-ring binders and writing tablets. They also sold patterns for making different and assorted clothing items, primarily ladies' clothes. Near the front was a long candy counter, rows of glass enclosed "aquarium like" areas for displaying all sorts of sweets, primarily of the hard candy variety. These glass candy counters were at just the right height for young boys to peer in and see the assortment of goodies in the offing. In the back of the store they had all sorts of potential pets for sale, including small turtles and hamsters. Also near the back were a couple of aisles with model kits for airplanes, ships and cars—which caught my fancy.

I purchased many models over the years at Danners and loved walking up and down the aisles to marvel at their collections. Some of the models I purchased include a working guillotine (my favorite) and caricatures of the Beatles. For a few years Danners had a model-making contest. Buy and assemble your model, submit it to the judges, have it displayed in the front window, and wait to see which model would be selected as winner. I entered the model making contest several times and can still remember my surprise and disappointment that I didn't win. My model making technique was perfect and I made no mistakes, or at least I thought as such. Near the checkout is where they displayed the phonograph records. I bought many 45's, which cost, I believe, thirty-five cents each—the Beatles, Peter and Gordon, Herman's Hermits, etc. Danners also had one of those squeaky wooden floors and that familiar smell that old buildings with wooden floors have. And if that weren't enough to earn Danners a place in my heart, my mother worked at Danners for a while before she married my dad and it's where she met one of her lifelong friends, Estelle Hendershot.

Dunkirk had three physicians in the '60s—Dr. Elizabeth Tate, Dr. Herbert Shroyer, and Dr. Charles Entner. Our family had always been patients of Dr. Tate, and her father before, Dr. Erwin C. Garber. As a young child, I visited, with much trepidation, Dr. Tate to get my required tetanus shots, polio, small pox, and other vaccinations. The waiting room was marked by an unfriendly antiseptic aroma, one which was most likely prevalent in all small doctor's offices. She had two small examination rooms in the back of her office, which was located on Main Street.

As a junior high school student and one who played sports, we were all required to get a yearly physical examination. Well, the modesty requirement of a twelve-year-old seventh grader when a woman physician is checking for a hernia and looking for any abnormal growths "down there" is, to say the least, important and tricky. Dr. Tate, in all her very subtle and kind ways, gracefully managed the examination by inspecting certain boy parts while I was partially clothed, thankfully avoiding a dreaded frontal "full Monty."

Unlike growing up in a big impersonal city, in a small Hoosier town like Dunkirk your personal experiences are impacted by the interesting small businesses and their owners. There was a woman's apparel store in town called The Cinderella Shop where my mother's friend Mabel Lefevre worked. Each Christmas I would enter the store with that deer in the eyes glazed look and tell Mabel I was buying my mother a Christmas present. She would gently guide me toward the women's slips or the women's handkerchiefs or something else I had no clue about and say, "I know she would like this." She would then gently put whatever I had agreed to in a box and beautifully wrap it and I was good to go. My mother always loved whatever I bought her for Christmas, be it a scarf or a knick-knack figurine from the little shop in the Todd Opera House building run by Anna Mae Fiddler.

Dunkirk was also home to Harrison's Green House, owned by brothers Paul and Brent Harrison. It was about two blocks from where I grew up and upon entering, was like walking into a different world, a sort of vegetative oasis of plants and flowers and humidity. Two full grown muscular boxers freely roamed Harrison's greenhouse and they were always a bit curious when someone entered—and a bit intimidating—so I did my best to keep an eye on them as I made my way through the jungle. The Harrison brothers, along with Brent's wife, ran the business and whenever I went there to buy my mother flowers for Mother's Day or her birthday, they always either gave me a great deal or gave them to me for free, telling me, "Your parents have always been so good to me, don't worry about it."

There was a permanent amusement park just one-and-a-half miles south, outside of Dunkirk on the state highway. This was a small amusement park owned by Eleanor Jane Garbor, who lived adjacent to the park. They had several kiddie rides with the most memorable being a small train that encircled the park. There was also a miniature golf course and merry-go-round and next to the park was a driving range that paralleled the highway. I only remember visiting the amusement park once, and it must have been when I was very young because all I can remember is being on a ride and having a blast, but it could have been more. It ceased operations in the mid '60s but its remains could be seen for decades.

There was a business called Lee's Men's Store that sold everything a man needed, from suits to dress shirts to ties to casual wear. Lee's Men's Store had it all. It was originated, owned and operated by Abraham (Abie) Glogas, an eastern European Jew who had immigrated to the U.S. from Poland in 1920 and who opened the store in 1935. Abie sold the store to his son Leo in 1962 but continued to be involved in its operation until 1970, when he passed away. Leo and his brother Gary continued to run the store for years and years. Leo was a very talkative and animated man who everyone loved and was an integral part of Dunkirk for decades. People loved stopping in to the store to find out what the latest goings on were in town or to share a story or to hear one of Leo's jokes. It was rumored that Leo knew the sizes of almost every customer who came into the store, so if you needed to buy a birthday present for your dad he made it easy. Leo's dressing room was in the rear of the store mixed in with his back stock and consisted of a curtain you pulled back for privacy. Conveniently, you could still converse with Leo while trying on pants or suits. Leo was also known to employ a variety of classic marketing techniques, passed on by his father Abie, I'm sure. One was that when times were lean and inventory a bit thin, he would stack empty shirt boxes in the showroom with a solitary shirt on the top, making it appear that the boxes were filled with other shirts.

Dunkirk's two drugstores were located practically across the street from each other. Shoemaker Drug Store, owned and operated by John Shoemaker, was on the corner of Main and Commerce Street. It had a side door and as you walked in, there was a counter where you could drop off your film for "speedy" processing—and pick it up a week later. Rawlings Drug Store, operated by Charles Rawlings, had a soda fountain, complete with counter and stools. As a young lad, I once went to Rawlings Drugs with a friend who had money for a bowl of ice cream. The soda jerk at the time, either J.T. or Bob Phillips, high school students, realized I didn't have any money and gave me a free scoop of ice cream. This act of kindness still resonates with me over fifty years later.

Watson's sporting goods was on Main Street just north of the railroad tracks. Run by Lou and Mary Lou Watson, the store had just about anything you'd want. My dad purchased my first set of golf clubs there in probably 1967 (I still use the putter). Each year, we would go in and look enviously at the baseball gloves and other equipment. They had tennis rackets, fishing poles, footballs, athletic apparel, just about anything sports related you would want. Watson's was also where the high school ordered class jackets and athletic jackets and athletic sweaters. The high school had requirements of how many Varsity letters you must earn to be awarded a green letter sweater and how many letters for a white letter sweater. There were also requirements for being awarded a DHS athletic jacket, the pinnacle of prestige in a small town. When I had finally met the requirements for getting a high school athletic jacket, I would stop in weekly to see if it had arrived, pestering Mary Lou, who was usually the one tending the store. When my jacket finally arrived, I was beyond happy and Mary Lou, I am sure, missed my visits.

At the other end of Main Street was Miss Ada Faulkner's little candy store, just a small room connected to the south of her house where we would buy candies on the way home from school. Pixie sticks, gumballs, jawbreakers—she had everything. Located strategically close to Westlawn and Sutton elementary schools, her shop was a favorite of all the kids not just for the sweets, but also sweet Miss Ada, an older lady who loved having us stop by.

Judy's drive-in was located on Center Street near the Armstrong Cork glass factory. It was a small house with the front room converted to a little store. We rode our bikes there to buy ice cream, primarily— what she called "frosties." Her little store also sold fireworks, and this is where we bought our bottle rockets and fire crackers.

The barber shop in a small town is, quite simply, a center for social and political opinion and commentary. It's where many of the world's problems are solved, many athletic teams critiqued, and many ideas bantered about that all affect this great country of ours. It's a place where men go to get their haircut, sure, but sometimes more importantly, to socialize with other men, tell jokes, make fun of each other, feel part of a group, or just loaf. My experience is that the conversations don't involve gossip and assuredly do not involve feelings. You would never walk into a barbershop and have someone say, "You look down today. Is everything all right? Tell me about it." (That is reserved for beauty salons.) It's where you go on Saturday to discuss Friday night's basketball game or find out what that siren last night was about.

The film *Hoosiers* had it right when it depicted the townspeople at the barber shop discussing the new coach. *The Andy Griffith Show* got it right with Floyd Lawson's shop being the place for congregating and for men to be with their friends. If a woman walked into the shop, most likely to bring her son to get a haircut, all conversation would cease immediately and an awkward silence would ensue.

In the '60s, there were two barbershops in Dunkirk—one, north of the railroad tracks, and the other, south of the tracks at the main intersection of downtown on Main Street and Commerce Street. Lloyd Anderson and Bill Shatto (and later, Jerry Friend) ran the shop north of the tracks. Bill Shatto then changed shops and with my uncle, Gary James, ran the one south of the tracks. In the late '60s a couple of young hotshot recent graduates of barber school took over the shop south of the tracks—Rod Hardwick and Dave Farmer have been cutting hair there ever since and I'm sure they have stories that could fill many books.

Every town has one: "Moon Man" Martin was a bit of a local character. Aptly named, Moon Man owned a small store about two blocks from the high school where we would go to buy Moon Pies or other snacks at lunch. Picture a rather small man wearing a pith helmet while inexplicably pushing a wheelbarrow about town—that was him. His house on Blackford Avenue was a bit of a mess and equally bizarre, the outside strewn with antennas and items for, I assume, monitoring space travel and any imminent landing of UFOs. What would life be like without such fascinating people?

Some of my best memories revolve around the Stewart Brothers furniture store in Dunkirk. Started in the late 1800s it had been in the family for three generations. My grandmother Marjorie (Stewart) Retter was one of the owners back in the '50s so it was only natural that my father, John Retter, work there. Dad was always handy so he attended carpet school in New York and ran the "carpet side" of the business for over 40 years. Dad and his carpet-laying partner, Grant Fager, were well respected for the quality work they did; in fact, I often told people, "My dad has probably been in every house in north-eastern Indiana." Don and Bob Stewart, for the most part, ran the store where they sold furniture, mattresses, floor covering, tables, and for a time, appliances and stereos. Don and Bob were both quite personable; thus, their market flourished beyond Dunkirk into numerous surrounding towns including Muncie and Hartford City.

I worked at the store delivering furniture the summer after graduating from high school with Jerry Nelson, a soft-spoken man with one fake eye who was a wonderful role model, mentor and friend. Jerry was in seminary at the time and wanted to be a minister. On a less holy note, he showed me the ropes of where to hide in the mattress balcony to take naps and how to avoid injury to my "man parts" while walking through a dark floor packed with furniture jutting out at a dangerous height just below the waist. Jerry also lifted weights and was quite strong, a useful characteristic to have in a furniture delivery partner when you're carrying a sleeper bed up or down a set of stairs. Other key players included Bob Jewel, master of fixing and assembling things at the store, who would occasionally help with deliveries. Then there was Mary Alice Ireland, a high school classmate of my parents who ran the office and, most likely, kept everyone in line. I was given no preferential treatment even though I was family; in fact, I told people I don't think my great uncle Don even knew my name because he always referred to me as "Hey, Umm," as in, "Hey, Umm, would you help move this table?"

Stewart Bros. Furniture

It's funny how seasons of our lives often center around the cars we drive. Cars always appear prominent in my childhood memories equal to the prominence of the car dealerships in our little town. Of the three new car dealers in Dunkirk—Leon Etchison Motors (in the late '60s it became Lowell Fuqua Motors Chrysler Plymouth), Crown City Chevrolet and Manor Brothers Ford—my father was a customer of the latter. Every two or three years, Dad would get a phone call from Bob Man-or telling him, "We've got a new car up here for you. I'll bring it by so you can take a look at it." Bob would bring the car over and let Dad drive it and, I imagine, sell him on the fact that it was time for a new one. Over the years, we owned two or three shiny new Galaxy 500 station wagons—the perfect vehicle to haul around two kids with a rear end that opened to let us sit either facing backwards or sometimes facing each other, depending on the car. The rear end opening was also handy in the winter when my father pulled us on our toboggans and saucers down a snowy Barbier Street just behind our house.

Every year the release of the new model cars was a big deal in Dunkirk. Local car dealers went to great lengths to hide the two or three new cars around town that they would eventually reveal to the public at the right time. In doing this, they would build suspense and add excitement to the process of the yearly new car model releases. As a kid, it was always a challenge and great fun to explore around town looking for a place the cars might be hidden. Sometimes we spotted a garage that had paper covering the windows, a clue that would lead us to find a nice shiny new car sitting inside. The payoff to us kids was when we visited each dealership on the Saturday morning of the great "reveal" and took advantage of the dealerships' offer of free doughnuts.

Another defining feature of small-town life was the local cinema. Dunkirk had a small movie theater in the early '60s called the Main Theater, which is where you'd find us on any given Saturday. Someone's parents would drop us off for the day to see a double feature for the low admission price of, I believe, thirty-five cents. For fifteen cents, we could splurge on popcorn. The double features often included an Elvis Presley film and periodically a 1950s "B" horror film. Back before reclining seats, or even carpet, the theaters had sloped cement floors, and more than once someone would knock over their empty glass soda bottle (we called all of them Coke bottles) and it would roll disruptively all the way to the front of the theater. Maintaining such a small theater and making money was, I'm sure, very difficult and time consuming, and with the opening of the Muncie Mall and discovery by Dunkirk residents of the Strand and Rivoli theaters in Muncie, Dunkirk's only theater closed and was torn down to make way for the new downtown bank building.

The Main Theater

Hometown Nicknames

WHETHER FOR AFFECTION OR RIDICULE, nicknames can create an emotional bond that can stick for life. I always pay attention when I hear them, because they can tell you interesting things about a person, often having a story attached to the name. And in my hometown, the number of people with nicknames seemed higher than the average per capita than elsewhere. These weren't just nicknames, either—they became the name of the person, and in most cases, I never even knew the "real" name of the individual.

Nicknames also were so ingrained that they sometimes appeared in the city's phone book! Giving nicknames may have been a generational thing for those born in the 1920s through 1950s. Or it could have been a small-town thing. Whatever the case, when my sister Connie and my uncle Gary and I got to discussing it one day, we were all amazed at how many people we grew up with who had nicknames. One of my school friends, "Chip" Phillips, was probably the first person I knew with a nickname. There was always a bit of confusion when at the start of the school year, Chip was identified as Tommy and we would always look at each other like, "Who the heck is Tommy Phillips?"

A few of the Dunkirk people I knew and remembered with nicknames include:

"Alkie" Shumaker
"Skud" Miller
"Skid" Woodard
"Dub" Miskinis
"Scoop" Campbell
"Checkie" Smith
"Chick" Whitesell
"Peanut" McEwen
"Pug" Norris
"Pee Wee" Thrash
"Speck" Morgan
"Curly" Wingate
"Fuzz" Barnum
"Red" Urick
"Curly" Fry
  Lots of "Buds"
"Moose" Hatch
"Sugarbear" Irelan
"Butch" Shroyer
"Chuck" Huffman

and the list goes on and on.

The Ornery Ones

AS BEST I CAN TELL, there were never two more ornery fellahs on the planet than my friends Rock Fuqua and Jeff Ford. They could probably be defined as quintessential ornery tricksters, always up to some shenanigans and characters to be rightly admired. Rock and Jeff not only were involved in many of our youthful high-jinx, but to this day can tell a story like no other, guaranteed to have you rolling around on the ground roaring with laughter. And right behind them on the honorable mention list of tricksters would be high school friends Larry Sampley, Vince Thompson, Doug Manor and Paul Hart, all with good senses of humor who enjoyed creating a good time in our small town. I'm proud to be included in this group of friends; we all had fun, gave each other a hard time, played practical jokes on each other, and grew as individuals together. Occasionally, we got in trouble together, because that's also what friends do.

All of us were basically good kids who all came from good families, but like normal young kids, we liked to dream up fun, and frequently crazy, and on occasion stupid, memorable "stuff" to do while in our teens—what some might call "pushing the envelope." It crosses my mind as to how some of the innocent shenanigans we did back then would be received today, in a larger town or a city, with perhaps less grace—especially without the support of loving parents and locals who knew who we were and who our parents were. I am proud to say that the "fun" we had didn't include drugs or guns or vandalism—things that seem to be more common in American culture today.

While decorum makes me hesitant to divulge too many of our youthful transgressions publicly (in addition to that statute of limitations thing, plus there are still parents living who might be inclined to "ground" the perpetrators, even though said perpetrators are in their fifties and sixties) or to put a name next to the mischief perpetrated, I hereto forth offer but a few of the "sort of" nefarious acts we committed in the name of fun:

- Throwing fish (i.e., bluegill) out the car window at other cars while driving down Main Street. I remember riding my bike down Main Street the next day and seeing flattened bluegill littering the street from one end to the next.

- Tossing a couple of large (approx. 5 pound) live fish, likely carp, into the local swimming pool in the spring before it opened for the season. Irreverently, the act was perpetrated between Easter sunrise service and regular service with one unnamed perpetrator going on to become a minister.

- Smoking cigars (Swisher Sweets) while driving around in our cars—our parents would have had our hides!

- Throwing walnuts at the hubcaps of passing cars while hiding in a ditch one Halloween. We got called on our little prank one time because one of our victims called the police, who dispatched a squad car to the area. Suddenly bright spotlights are sweeping the woods where we were crouched down trying to hide behind trees, in bushes, under leaves, some of us in a trailer even. I think this is the most scared I've ever been in my entire life.

- Hunting rabbits with shotguns, which, due to not actually getting any rabbits, led to the hunting of sparrows. We hunted on Thanksgiving and during Christmas break and though we rarely saw anything to hunt, we loved being outside in the cold weather all bundled up walking through recently plowed fields.

- Smoking more cigars (more Swisher Sweets).

- Sleeping out in the yard and ... smoking cigars. Just us, in our sleeping bags, under the stars, in the front yard of a friend's house on Main Street. The cigars we smoked were of the "very large" variety and I remember the next morning my eyes were almost swollen shut from the smoke.

- Sleeping in the cemetery. This had always been on the list of "We need to do this sometime" and we did it—in a small isolated cemetery west of Dunkirk. There were three or four of us and our car was parked in the cemetery. Surprisingly, it was not scary at all as we were all too tired to care. I can't believe none of the farmers who drove by the cemetery the next morning didn't report the car to police. Or maybe they did.

- Soaping windows on Halloween. A classic fun thing to do; my parents allowed me to soap the car and house windows after I asked permission, and my father would always say, "As long as you don't tear anything up."

- Throwing corn onto the rooftops and porches of houses on Halloween. With ample field corn not yet harvested in late October, it was always easy to get a few ears of corn to shuck and use for mischievous activities such as throwing onto rooves—especially metal rooves, which made a nice loud clatter when they landed.

Let this be my public apology for said pranks but also let it be known, all this orneriness was not hateful or destructive and never resulted in injury to people or property. We never felt the pangs of guilt for what we did—just a sense of adventure and the kind of adrenalin-focused feeling like this may just be our last chance to grab life before we have to grow up.

The Progressing of Life

TODAY IT'S A LITTLE EASIER keeping in touch with my old friends and buddies from growing up. The magic of the Interweb, and particularly Facebook, has made it almost too simple. Prior to these wondrous methods of communication, however, people most likely would simply drop off the face of the earth, never to be heard from again. Everyone would just sort of go off in their own direction and that was that.

For me, the experiences I've had and the relationships I've known can be categorized into three different stages of life. The first stage was my childhood growing up in a small town. A time and a place in life when my parents were always there... where I always had classmates and neighbor friends around me... where I knew my parents' friends and where almost everyone knew my parents... where I had a large pool of friends, the same people who I spent hours with in class, in sports, in clubs ... and who grew up with me and lived life together from first grade through twelfth grade.

The second phase of life was marked by a transition from all that I knew in my small hometown of Dunkirk. After graduating from high school, I immediately lost almost every high school and small town relationship that had kept me safe and gave me comfort. I left town to attend college and was thrown into a new environment that required I take care of myself, figure out what needed to be done myself, and meet new people from all over the United States and even other countries. The number of friends I had decreased dramatically, but were still important as we were all going through that growing up phase together, trying to figure out about the world and where we fit in.

Phase three includes the time after I left college to enter the real world, where friends are determined by who you work with and, to a lesser degree, who your neighbors are. Subsequent phases are pretty much a derivation of the third phase and occur as you move to different houses or cities, take on new jobs because of promotions, attend and meet people at church, participate in athletic or other activities.

Despite all the changes and transitions and seasons of life, the one constant I've known through it all is family. My family has always been there and always will be—until of course they pass away or perhaps move away. But, for good or bad (for me, good), family will always be my foundation. There will always be holiday dinners and birthdays and get-togethers. Family are the ones who will always remember stories about you from your youth that you don't remember. They will always be around to ask about something from the past, to help you remember what is important—your parents, your beginnings, your traditions, your life.

Small Town Indiana Redux

WHAT IT MEANS TO LIVE in small town Indiana has changed greatly over the years. Population masses have migrated to the larger cities where service jobs, entertainment jobs, technical jobs, and non-manufacturing positions exist. The automotive industry has changed dramatically the past thirty to forty years, bringing with it plant closings or businesses moving to other areas of the country, or world for that matter, and with that, residual companies that supply parts and services to the larger plants. Industries have consolidated. Small businesses have dissipated and people now rely more on 'big box" stores for their hardware, clothing, and food needs. Businesses are more apt to be a franchise of a larger company with people working in the local stores being paid lower wages. People are looking for cheaper goods and services and so "dollar" stores and big box stores have flourished. People are more willing to drive twenty or even 100 miles to do their shopping, or buy online. Small towns have suffered throughout the United States.

Schools have also consolidated into larger entities with a goal of giving students better educational opportunities and reducing overall expenses through economies of scale. And while consolidation provides some benefits, it also takes away opportunities for some. Not all students in larger schools can participate in athletics as in smaller schools. Students don't get to know all their classmates and learn from them, for better or for worse. Students don't get the luxury of knowing other students' parents and having them be an influence in their lives. Students are not as likely to grow a special lifelong bond with their classmates and have a special feeling of warmth toward their school. Consolidation tends to take away a town's pride and eliminates that central location to congregate, a very important ingredient to people's need to belong.

Smaller towns now tend to be populated by retired individuals, commuters, artists and people who exist on fewer amenities. My hometown has experienced this change. Small businesses have closed, people have passed away and moved away, management from the local glass industry no longer live locally, and some buildings are empty. Inexpensive illegal drugs have seeped into the culture, cheap unhealthy foods permeate menus, and it seems "quickie marts" are the only place to get a meal. I've lived during a time of the evolution of small towns and the migration of wealth into larger cities.

And while I've seen a lot of changes in the small town I grew up the '60s, the thing I've observed and experienced is that considering this evolution, the small-town spirit still exists and is going strong, thank you very much! Good people are still there, people are still friendly, people are still kind, people still care about each other, people want to help, people want to volunteer, people want to provide, people want to belong.

I believe we all, in some way, still wish we lived in a small town...that unique environment, somewhat like Mayberry, where everyone knows everyone else. Where you can walk everywhere without jumping into your car. Where you know the owners of the small businesses you frequent. Where you know the servers by their first names. Where you know your neighbors and hang out with them. That feeling of being connected. Of being known.

The sentimentality and warmth of my small town comes flooding back to me whenever I attend the Dunkirk High School alumni banquet, where everyone who EVER attended the high school is invited. I see friendships that have existed for forty, fifty, sixty years and I see how important these friendships are. I see people I haven't seen in sometimes, forty years, but when I revive that relationship, it's as if we haven't missed a beat and can pick up right where we left off.

For me, reminiscing is a wonderful way of feeling connected and a reminder of how safe I felt while growing up. Several friends of mine who grew up in larger cities and attended large schools shared that they have no connection with their childhood. They may have gotten a bit better high school education or they may have been exposed to some other aspects of life not experienced in a small town, but, by golly, growing up in a small town, to me, is just one of the most precious things I could have been blessed with. And my small town produced an awful lot of successful people, from teachers to surgeons to lawyers to business owners to skilled factory workers to bankers. Heck, it even produced some goofball guy whose goal it was to write a book about his experiences of growing up.

The Other Phone Call

THIS ONE CAME IN ON a Sunday morning in October, four months and a few days after my sister had called me on that Monday in June about my mother being taken to the hospital.

Again, I can't remember what I was doing, but I recall my sister in a broken voice saying, "It's your dad. You need to come home right away."

Going Home

UNEXPECTEDLY LOSING BOTH PARENTS FOUR months apart is a tough pill to swallow. Suddenly, my foundation was shaken, the rug pulled out from underneath me. My parents had always made me feel grounded, always gave me a place to return to, were always there. Just as they were when I had a track meet or a basketball game or Parents' Day at Purdue. They were always available if I had a question about something, sometimes mundane, sometimes trivial. Oh sure, they fussed with each other later in life and listened carefully as the other told a story, making sure it was accurate and correcting when it wasn't—which was often. Toward the end, our conversations seemed to always include the weather and body aches and pains, as expected for a couple who had been married for almost 56 years.

When they were still with us, the house I grew up in, the room I grew up in, however, had always been available to me— still decorated with my boyhood trophies and posters and jerseys. It wasn't until I was in my fifties that my mother gave me an ultimatum: "You need to go through those drawers in your

bedroom and take what is yours, because I … need the space."
I think it was difficult for her to ask me to chuck my stuff; after
all, your mother doesn't stop being your mother just because
you're grown up. But it was time for me to see my mom as an
adult who didn't need to be responsible for my stuff. Finally,
it was time to get rid of my old high school gym shorts and
t-shirts I stored there "in case of an emergency." (I can't imagine any emergency requiring the sudden need to wear my high
school gym clothes.) Only a few years earlier she had told me
to "go through that box of models in the closet and take what
you want. The rest I'm going to throw out, because I … need
the space."

And so it goes that the ranch house I grew up in and the
friendly hometown I knew so well was going to change whether
I liked it or not, and whether I was ready for it or not. My parents were gone. My home sweet home would soon be gone. My
Dunkirk connection that had always been there whether it was
visits on holidays and other special events was going away. So
was the bedroom where I had lain awake at night, wondering if I
would make the varsity basketball team or not. The living room
where I lay on the floor watching "Mr. Ed" and "Voyage to the
Bottom of the Sea" and "The Rat Patrol" and "Lost in Space."
The basement where a gazillion raucous games of pool and ping
pong had been played and where Rock Fuqua and I played ping
pong with double or nothing stakes (I think I still owe him a
couple hundred thousand dollars). The car port where as a
young owner of a go-kart I crashed into the milk box and broke
the empty glass milk bottle and got into trouble. The driveway

where my basketball goal was located and where I painted the free-throw line and jump ball line, all per spec.

All those wonderful memories and experiences would still be in my mind, but I would only be able to drive by on Broad Street and see the house wistfully from afar… or so I thought. Fortunately for me, my sister still lived in Dunkirk. She worked at the local bank and was still very active in the community, and unbeknownst to me, she had no intentions of selling the house as part of my parents' estate; she wanted to keep it. She would move down the street a few blocks on Broad Street and into the house my father built in 1958. I was one very lucky person. The house I lived in for almost all my formative years would remain in the family. The house where we stood around the phonograph in 1963 and listened to the Beatles' vinyl forty-fives, "She Loves You, (Ya Ya Ya)" and "I Want to Hold Your Hand." It would be more than a place I would simply drive by and look at with fond memories. It would continue to be filled with our family and our life.

My sister moved into the house soon after my parents passed away and, to her credit, she made some very nice improvements. She updated the carpet, expanded the master bathroom, changed wallpaper, had a garage built, removed the crumbling front patio. All things to make her feel like it was hers. It looks great and I'm impressed and proud of her for doing such a fine job. And I'm happy to say I can still visit any time I want.

And so, like everything, the house I grew up in and the small town I grew up in has changed for sure. But hasn't every place?

And hasn't everyone? As I drive down Moore Avenue and onto Broad Street toward the house, I still pass by Fulkersons' house where I spent so much time playing basketball. And when I drive by the Pine Patch and Shumakers' house and Millers' house, I look and remember the times years ago when an innocent young boy played with neighbors and I flash back to all the good, safe times spent there in the peace and tranquility of this friendly town.

Today the face of Dunkirk looks quite different. The trees have all grown taller and thicker; some trees have simply disappeared. Some of the houses don't look that familiar to me anymore; old wooden siding has been replaced with modern vinyl or rooms have been added to expand existing homes or in some cases houses have been razed. All this change after fifty years gets me thinking: What is it that makes us who we are? Are we shaped by the places we live? And why is it that certain times of our lives are so important? And why do we hold certain memories and experiences so dear? For me, the answers are not clear but somehow it all goes back to a time long ago, to a boy of just five years old and his first memories of experiences in a small town called Dunkirk and the life that would unfold there. And I am thankful for growing up a small-town Hoosier.

The End

61874274R00086

Made in the USA
Lexington, KY
23 March 2017